MW00559437

GARDEN GROWN

GARDEN GROWN

Julia Dzafic
with Anel Dzafic
Photography by Julia D'Agostino

Publisher Mike Sanders
Art & Design Director William Thomas
Editorial Director Ann Barton
Senior Editor Olivia Peluso
Designer Studio Noel
Photographer Julia D'Agostino
Food Stylist Nicolette Massaro
Recipe Tester Dana Angelo White
Compositor Ayanna Lacey
Proofreaders Christina Guthrie & Mira S. Park
Indexer J. Bradley Herrimann

First American Edition, 2024
Published in the United States by DK Publishing
1745 Broadway, 20th Floor, New York, NY 10019

The authorized representative in the EEA is Dorling Kindersley
Verlag GmbH. Arnulfstr. 124, 80636 Munich, Germany

Copyright © 2024 by Julia Dzafic
DK, a Division of Penguin Random House LLC
23 24 25 26 27   10 9 8 7 6 5 4 3 2 1
001–339559–May/2024

All rights reserved.
Without limiting the rights under the copyright reserved
above, no part of this publication may be reproduced, stored
in or introduced into a retrieval system, or transmitted, in any
form, or by any means (electronic, mechanical, photocopying,
recording, or otherwise), without the prior written permission
of the copyright owner.

A catalog record for this book
is available from the Library of Congress.
ISBN 978-0-7440-9303-2

DK books are available at special discounts when purchased
in bulk for sales promotions, premiums, fund-raising, or
educational use. For details, contact SpecialSales@dk.com

Printed and bound in China

www.dk.com

MIX
Paper | Supporting
responsible forestry
FSC™ C018179

This book was made with Forest
Stewardship Council™ certified
paper – one small step in DK's
commitment to a sustainable future.
Learn more at
www.dk.com/uk/information/sustainability

To Amalia and Luca. You are my sunshine.

Contents

From Seedlings to Garden

My husband, Anel, and I couldn't come from more different backgrounds. While he was surviving a war in Bosnia as a child, I was living in a small New England town where the idea of war was just that: an idea. And one that felt very far away. It's a small miracle that we ended up finding each other to create such a beautiful life.

Anel was born in a village outside of Banja Luka, Bosnia, then Yugoslavia. When he was only seven years old, a horrifying genocide and war broke out all around him. While I remember reading about it in school, Anel was living it.

He heard the bombs going off at night. He watched his uncles get sent away to concentration camps. His father hid in the woods behind the family home day in and day out to avoid being taken away to dig trenches for the other side. My husband watched as his country, his family, and his life were ripped apart. He witnessed far more devastation than any little boy should ever have to see.

Food was rationed, but his family survived in part due to their farm and garden. He learned how undeniably crucial food can be when you don't have enough of it.

At the end of the war, Anel and his parents were miraculously able to get out of Bosnia and immigrate to the United States. They were immigrants. They were Muslim. They didn't speak a word of English.

He walked onto his first airplane ride ever with only the backpack on his back, leaving his entire world for a foreign country. They landed in Queens with no work and no money, but lots of hope for the future. Anel taught himself English by watching TV shows the summer before he started school.

Over the course of the next two decades, he worked hard to learn a new language, graduating from high school a semester early. He followed his passion for healthy living by becoming a personal trainer and health coach. Today, he owns a successful fitness studio in Greenwich, Connecticut, where he and his trainers work with an elite clientele. My husband has overcome adversity and stereotypes; he is literally living the American dream as an entrepreneur, doing what he loves every day.

He spends much of his free time outside. He takes great pride in tending to our family garden and taking care of our ten chickens. Because his childhood garden was such a huge part of his life and crucial for his family's survival, his love for gardening has deep roots. Every time he brings in a bountiful harvest, he has a huge smile on his face.

My story took a very different path. I grew up in Hanover, New Hampshire, an Ivy League college town where my parents were both professors. There was food on the table every night—and then some. I never once worried about where my next meal would come from.

I always had an itch to explore the world, so I somehow convinced my parents to let me go to high school in Rome, Italy. From there, I went to college in Southern California and studied abroad in Florence. I loved—and still love—Italy, and I learned so much about food and cooking from my time there.

I was never satisfied with my traditional jobs after college. They didn't fulfill me creatively in the way that I somehow, deep down, knew I needed. I went back to school to become a health coach and started working with clients on their nutrition and lifestyle while working in marketing during the day to pay the bills. I met Anel at work. In fact, I was his boss!

At this point, I really started experimenting in the kitchen, trying every new vegetable I could get my hands on. I learned how to massage kale for salads, how to create a deep umami flavor, and how to develop my own recipes for the first time.

In 2010, I started Lemon Stripes, a blog where I shared these recipes along with healthy tips for my clients, friends, and family. I would post the recipes on my personal Facebook page (the only social media platform at the time), and every week, more people would look at my posts.

As my blog grew, I began to write about other aspects of my life. The more I opened up, the more young women related to it in a bigger way. During this time, Anel and I fell in love. We got married two years later.

When Instagram came to town, I started using it right away and was able to grow my following quickly. This growth helped to grow my blog in turn, and it's been flowing in that direction ever since.

In 2016, I quit my full-time, in-house marketing job. I was completely burned out from working 90-hour weeks on both my "real" work and Lemon Stripes. It was scary, but taking that leap of faith is one of the best decisions I've ever made.

A year later, Anel and I had our first baby, our daughter, Amalia, and moved to our dream house in Connecticut. Four years later, we had our son, Luca.

During the pandemic, Anel built a giant, beautiful garden that kept him busy and calm during a very dark time. I quickly realized that I would have to get creative in the kitchen with all of the extra produce he was bringing in seemingly every day. I learned how to pickle, how to make sauces, and how to use herbs in new and exciting ways.

I started sharing these concoctions online and soon found myself overwhelmed with questions from readers about what to do with extra tomatoes, cucumbers, and peppers. And so, this book was born. I hope the recipes inspire you to get creative with all of your homegrown produce, too.

You'll also find a treasure trove of gardening tips from Anel, a man who knows how to plant, harvest, water, and fertilize each plant front to back. We have come together to create this book out of a love for good (yet easy-to-make) recipes, fresh veggies straight from the earth, and each other. We hope you love it!

How to Use This Book

There are 108 recipes in this book, all of them created with love. The recipes are organized into nine chapters based on different fruits and vegetables from the garden. If you're looking for something to cook with an overload of tomatoes, make your way to the tomato chapter (pages 209 to 234). Overflowing in peppers? Check out the pepper chapter (pages 211 to 235)! Most recipes are plant-forward, but you'll also find meat and fish options throughout.

Each chapter begins with gardening tips from Anel to maximize your harvest and an "offshoot" recipe, which is a fun new way to make or store that ingredient. You'll find a recipe for herbed salt (see page 135) in the herbs chapter, three easy pickle recipes (see page 53) in the cucumber chapter, and much more.

To help you make the most of your garden bounty, most recipes include a "cross-pollination" section, a visual way for you to see which ingredients from other chapters you might be able to pull from your garden. For example, my vegetarian chili recipe (see page 222) is in the pepper chapter; its cross-pollination section has an herb icon and an onions & garlic icon to showcase those ingredients.

I encourage you to have fun while cooking, play around with the recipes, and enjoy every last bite of your bounty!

 Tomatoes

 Cucumbers

 Leafy Greens

 Eggplant

 Herbs

 Onions & Garlic

 Carrots

 Peppers

 Berries

Anel's

Gardening Basics

Building a Garden

The most important thing to think about is location. Most vegetables require six to eight hours of direct sunlight each day, so your garden's location makes a big difference. You can build traditional in-ground beds or raised beds, or you can use simple containers. It doesn't have to be complicated!

When you find the perfect sunny location, think about the pests around that may damage your garden. For example, in the Northeast, fighting off deer is a daily occurrence. Having a fenced-in garden is extremely important for a successful harvest.

If you're growing berries, think about netting or fencing, to prevent birds from gobbling up all of your hard work. I don't mind sharing with the animals, but unfortunately, they don't want to share with me very often.

Designing a Garden

Taking the time to design your garden layout will maximize space and provide healthy plant growth. I usually do this in the off-season.

First, think about the accessibility of your garden beds. You should be able to walk around the beds or rows easily for planting, weeding, and harvesting without stepping on the soil around the plants.

Next, plan for plants with similar needs (water, nutrients, sunlight) to be together for easier maintenance. For example, I plant my lettuce between my tomatoes or peppers, because leafy greens thrive in shade.

When you run out of room or soil to grow vegetables, consider vertical gardening as well. I use trellises, cages, and stakes to support tomatoes, cucumbers, and beans. These maximize your space and prevent overcrowding.

My garden is its own little ecosystem. It's very important to incorporate flowers into the design, because flowering plants attract pollinators like bees and butterflies. These insects play a crucial role in pollinating crops, which leads to better fruit and higher yields. Some flowers attract

predators that can help control pests naturally, too. For example, marigolds give off a strong scent that acts as a natural pest repellent. Plus, they're beautiful!

Prepping the Soil

Soil prep is crucial for creating a healthy environment for your vegetables to thrive in.

Start by testing your soil's pH levels. You can find kits at your local garden center or through a local agricultural experiment station. The ideal pH for soil is 6.5, but anywhere between 5.5 and 7.5 is okay.

If your soil's pH balance is below 5.5, adding lime will raise the pH levels. If your levels are over 7.5, add sulfur or other acidifying materials, like peat moss, to lower the pH. Whenever you bring up the balance in your soil, allow it to rest for at least a week before planting, as this gives your newest application time to integrate with the existing soil.

Next, remove weeds, rocks, or debris from the area to provide a clean space for planting. Once you have your soil test results, you can determine what is needed to improve your soil quality pH and nutrient content.

Finally, add in compost (more on page 18) to improve the soil's structure and nutrient retention. Aim for 2 to 3 inches of compost matter on top of the soil.

Planting

It's very important to purchase seedlings from a good source. I highly recommend going to a local nursery, which will sell plants that will thrive in your growing zone. Look for seedlings that feel sturdy, have healthy leaves, and show no signs of disease or pests. Before buying, I take each plant out of its container to see what the roots look like. If it's root-bound (it has too many roots and looks like it's trying to escape the container), I try to find another seedling.

Plant seedlings outdoors when the danger of frost has passed. If you plant your seedlings too early and one final frost appears, it will stop the growth of your vegetables or potentially eliminate them completely.

After you bring them home, keep your seedlings inside until they're ready to be planted. Seedlings often need time to acclimate to outdoor conditions. Place your seedlings outdoors in a sheltered area for a few hours, and each day gradually increase their exposure to light and outdoor temperatures. Plant them in the ground in 7 to 10 days. This helps avoid shock, which can prevent the plant from growing at a normal pace. We gardeners get very excited in early spring to get things planted, but these tiny adjustments can dictate the success of your garden.

Once the plants are acclimated and ready to be planted permanently, choose a day that's partly cloudy (or a sunny late afternoon) for planting to reduce transplant shock.

For each plant, dig a hole that is slightly larger than the root ball of your seedling. Remove the seedling from the container, being very careful not to damage the roots. Turn the container upside down, and with the plant in between your fingers, gently tap the bottom of the container until the plant is loose and about to fall out. Don't pull the plant from the stem out of the container; it will break. Place the seedling in the hole and backfill it with soil. To eliminate air pockets, gently pat the soil down around the stem.

Each seedling should come with instructions and recommendations on planting and spacing. Proper spacing will eliminate overcrowding and ensure there is enough air circulation between your plants.

When all of your seedlings are planted, add a layer of organic mulch around them to help retain moisture, suppress weeds, and regulate soil temperatures. I usually use straw, but wood chips work as well.

Watering

One of the most important parts of growing vegetables is adequate watering. A plant will tell you when it needs to be watered; it will look sad, with droopy leaves that are starting to turn brown. I find watering very meditative and grounding, and I love going out to water my babies. That said, the best money I've spent in a long time was on an irrigation system to ensure that I never miss a day of watering, which is especially crucial in the hot New England summers.

In the spring, my irrigation goes off 20 minutes per day. Mid-summer, it's an hour per day, usually in the mornings. At the end of the summer, when it's extremely humid and hot in the Northeast, it waters for an hour in the morning and an hour in the evening.

If you don't have a drip irrigation system, use a regular garden hose or soaker hose.

Fertilizing

Start by testing your soil to determine what nutrients it needs and what the pH levels are. Balanced fertilizers, with equal ratios of nitrogen, phosphorus, and potassium, are great for most vegetables.

Think about adjusting the ratios based on the growth stage of your vegetables. For example, use higher phosphorus for flowering veggies. Plants may need additional phosphorus and potassium. It's very simple: Just follow the instructions on the label of the fertilizer.

Midway through the growing season, lightly scatter some organic fertilizer or compost around the plants to replenish nutrients. As the vegetables grow, they will take nutrients from the soil, so it's important to replenish them.

Avoid over-fertilizing. Too much fertilizer will throw off the balance in your soil. Some vegetables may overgrow and become a complete mess. Some vegetables have different nutrient needs, so you might need to separate them. For example, I have my berry patch separate from my vegetable garden, because berries like an acidic fertilizer. Plan your own garden accordingly.

Pests

Pest control involves a combination of preventative measures, monitoring the garden, and intervention. And try to remember that if you have bugs, it means you have plants worth eating!

Prevent

Prevention begins with healthy soil. When your soil is strong, your crops will be more resistant to pests.

Companion planting is a great natural form of pest control. Certain plants repel pests and attract helpful insects. For example, planting basil in your garden will repel aphids, pests that suck sap from your plants, preventing them from fully maturing. Marigold is another great pest-repeller that also attracts ladybugs, which control any aphid infestation. Plus, it's beautiful to look at!

Another easy form of pest control is simply cleaning your garden by removing fallen leaves and weeds where pests can hide and breed.

Monitor

Monitor the garden to see if there are any signs of damage to leaves, such as holes, wilting, or discolored spots. Remove damaged leaves so that the plant can focus on supporting the healthy leaves and fruit.

If you notice flying insects, such as white flies or Japanese beetles, put in yellow sticky traps, pheromone traps, or even simple white netting (if you don't mind the look of it), to monitor and capture them. You may need to get your hands dirty and handpick caterpillars, slugs, or snails off of your plants.

Intervene

Inviting natural predators to the garden is a great intervention tactic. I plant specific plants to attract ladybugs, lacewings, and wasps to feed on garden pests.

Neem oil is an organic solution that disrupts the lifecycle of many pests, but you have to apply it every other day for it to work. If you have an infestation, and you need a quick cleanup, a mixture of mild dish soap and water can suffocate insects like aphids and mites. If that fails, try an organic insecticide. Bonide makes a great range of chemical-free options for organic gardening.

Harvesting

Harvesting vegetables at the right time is important to ensure that they're as flavorful and nutritious as possible. If you purchase your seedlings from a nursery, they will provide an accurate timeframe of when your vegetables will be ready for harvest. Keep those table labels, especially when you're growing something new.

Most vegetables taste the best when harvested at peak ripeness, but sometimes that's not an option, especially if you have squirrels or chipmunks around. As soon as I see some red on my tomatoes, they come off the vine. Otherwise, I wouldn't have a single tomato in my garden. I place my tomatoes in a fruit bowl on the counter, as most fruits, especially bananas, produce a hormone called ethylene, which helps the ripening process.

Harvest vegetables in the morning when possible, because that's when they are the freshest and the temperatures are cooler. For many vegetables, like sugar snap peas, tomatoes, and peppers, you can simply twist or gently pull, and the fruit will come off the plant. For vegetables with thicker stems, use pruning shears or scissors.

To harvest root vegetables, loosen up the soil around the roots and work your way down using your hands. Avoid digging tools, as they can easily damage root vegetables.

For leafy greens and herbs, work from the outside in. Harvest outer leaves first and work your way in toward the root. Toward the end of the season, you can harvest the whole head of lettuce, spinach, or kale.

End of Season

Once I'm done with my final harvest, I aerate the soil with a pitchfork very gently so as not to disturb the organisms living within it, lay down a few inches of compost, and cover it all up with mulch leaves that I get from around the property. This off-season soil prep is important for success the next season, so don't skip it. During the off-season, I plan out the garden layout for the following year, since everything is still fresh in my mind.

By following these tips and staying ahead of the game, you will increase your chances of success for the following season!

What to Do When You Grow Too Much

Food waste might not seem like that big of a deal in your home, but in most developed countries, over half of food waste actually happens at home.[1]

In fact, about one third of the food that is intended for human consumption every year (around 1.3 billion tons) is wasted or lost. This is enough to feed 3 billion people! Think those numbers are shocking? Check out these food waste facts:[2]

- The water used to produce the food wasted could be used by 9 billion people at around 200 liters per person per day.
- Food loss and waste accounts for about 4.4 gigatons of greenhouse gas emissions annually.
- If food loss were a country, it would be the third-largest greenhouse gas emitter, behind China and the US.
- If 25 percent of the food currently being wasted globally were saved, it would be enough to feed 870 million people around the world.

You're probably asking yourself what you, one person, can do about this. Well, I am a big believer that every small step adds up to make a bigger difference, and I have five steps that you can take at home to help prevent food waste.

Step 1: Smarter Shopping

It all starts at the grocery store: Plan to shop smarter. I like to make a list divided by area of the grocery store: produce, aisles, and frozen sections. Before making the list, I check to see which ingredients we've run out of and what we need for meals in the upcoming week. Including quantities is important, too. If I just write "onions" on the list, I might end up with four or five when I only need two.

If I go into the grocery store with no plan, I'll end up buying a ton of things I don't need, and those things may ultimately end up getting wasted.

Step 2: Fridge Storage

One thing that has helped us a ton is what I call fridge prep. When I buy or grow fresh fruits and veggies for snacking and cooking, I immediately put them into glass storage containers so they're easy to find in the fridge.

In the past, we would harvest kale or carrots, store them in the veggie drawer, and then forget about them. All of that hard work of growing veggies for nothing!

I now use the drawers for things that I know we'll go through daily and I'll never forget about, like bread and eggs. It goes against every beautiful fridge photo ever, but it works for us.

The other important piece to this puzzle is properly storing fruits and veggies to last longer. I make sure to always wash and dry everything before storing. I bought produce keepers online and found that berries, greens, and carrots last a lot longer. To store herbs, I wrap the stems in wet paper towels.

Step 3: Meal Prep

Along with grocery store planning, this is probably the most important step in not wasting food in our house. I cook a family meal for dinner about four times per week and always make extra for lunch leftovers. That leaves one weekday of ordering in or buying prepared meals.

To plan meals, I save recipes to Pinterest and look through my favorite cookbooks (like this one!) and blogs (like Lemon Stripes!) for inspiration.

1. "Food waste facts to motivate you to waste less," Olio, accessed October 9, 2023, https://olioapp.com/en/waste-and-our-planet/food-waste-facts-to-motivate-you-to-waste-less/.

2. Deena Robinson, "25 Shocking Facts About Food Waste," Earth.org, last modified September 29, 2023, https://earth.org/facts-about-food-waste/.

Anel and I look through the plan for the week on Sunday nights, and once we're both on board, I make the shopping list and shop on Mondays. This doesn't always work out perfectly, but it's our goal to do this as much as possible.

Step 4: Backstock of Pantry Items

I can meal prep until the cows come home, but there will always be extra veggies in our fridge that go to waste unless I get creative. In the summer, I throw together salads (like My Favorite Summer Salad on page 34) and in the fall and winter, I either do a big veggie roast or a soup (like Creamy Dairy-Free Tomato Soup on page 46). This happens about once a week, usually toward the end of the week when I really feel like ordering dinner but try to think about what I can make with what I have instead.

An essential part of this step is having pantry items and spices stocked up so that I have more recipe options for leftover veggies.

I always keep a backstock of at least three of every ingredient we use regularly. The top items in our backstock are Rao's tomato sauce, canned diced tomatoes, tomato paste, chicken and veggie broth, cannellini beans, black beans, chickpeas, olive oil, green chiles, canned tuna, pasta, and salsa.

I also try to keep chicken breast and ground beef or turkey in the fridge so that meatballs or chili are just a step away.

Step 5: Composting

At the end of the day, there's always going to be some food waste in our house, and that may be the case in your home as well. Composting at least some of that waste cuts it down big time and gives it back to the ground.

Composting is good for the environment for a whole host of reasons:

It decreases food waste: Not only do our leftover food scraps not end up in the trash, but we're able to recycle them from our own home. It feels really good to see how much less trash we have now.

It cuts out chemical fertilizers: Compost is a natural fertilizer that returns nutrients to our soil. It will (hopefully) lead to better yields in the garden so we can buy even less produce at the grocery store.

It cuts down on greenhouse gas: Organic waste that breaks down in landfill sites produces harmful greenhouse gas emissions, but home composting does not.[3]

What You Need for Composting

Inside: We have a small compost bucket that lives on our kitchen counter. We fill it up every few days and then bring it out to the larger one outside.

Outside: We have a large tumbling composter that lives behind our garden. We chose a tumbler because it's easier to tumble than it is to hand turn. Anel turns it five or six times every two days and whenever he adds something new to it. The one we chose also has two compartments so you can make two batches at once.

One side can be "cooking" as you add to the other. But the most important thing to look out for is something that will keep rodents out. Ours is lifted off the ground so the chance of small animals getting in is pretty low. Even better, it's made from 100 percent post-consumer recycled waste.

Compost starter: Anel used soil and worms that he found in the garden to start ours, but a store-bought compost starter is helpful if you don't have soil or worms readily available.

Brown vs. Green Matter

When you compost, you want to keep the ratio of two parts brown matter to one part green matter. This ratio can change depending on who you ask and the climate where you live. Let me explain...

What is brown compost? Brown materials are high in carbon and a good source of energy for the microbes found in compost.

Examples of brown compost include:

- Sticks, twigs, and tree bark
- Leaves
- Pine needles
- Corn stalks
- Sawdust
- Paper and cardboard (We stay away from newspaper, because it's chemically treated.)

What is green compost? Green compost consists mostly of wet materials or materials that were recently growing. Green materials are usually green or come from plants that were green at some point.

Examples of green compost include:

- Coffee grounds
- Banana peels and apple cores
- Eggshells
- Fruit and veggie scraps
- Grass
- Teabags

---

3. Carolyn Fry, "Tread lightly: Compost organic waste," *The Guardian*, April 17, 2008, https://www.theguardian.com/environment/ethicallivingblog/2008/apr/18/compostorganicwaste.

What not to compost:

- Fish or meat scraps
- Bones
- Dairy products
- Fat, grease, and oils
- Pet waste
- Grass or leaves treated with chemicals
- Diseased plants

Nurture It

Keep an eye on your compost and make sure your ratios are right. If you have too much green, the compost will start to smell. If you have too much brown, it will get too dry. Anel adds soil and water as needed to move it along.

How Long Does It Take?

It can take anywhere from one to four months to make a usable compost pile. The warmer the weather, the faster it goes. It can also take some time to figure out your ratios, but once you get that down, it will move faster. You'll know when to take it out when it's a dark brown color, looks like dirt, smells earthy, and crumbles in your hand.

How to Use Your Compost

Once your compost is fully cured, use it to replenish the nutrients in your soil by applying 2 to 3 inches of compost on top of your soil. At the beginning of the season, it will give your new seedlings extra nutrients for better root development. If you apply it in the middle of the season, it will encourage your vegetables to develop strong and healthy fruit. At the end of the season, applying compost increases your garden's chances of success for the following year.

The leftover food that we eat in our home goes into the composter, which turns into soil, which in turn gives nutrients to our plants, which we then eat. It's a pretty amazing circle of life right in our own backyard!

Off-Season Storage

Garden season in New England ranges from May to October, but we like to enjoy the fruits of Anel's labor year-round. I've taught myself a few tricks to make this happen. And guess what? They're a lot easier than you might think!

Pickling

I become a pickle monster at the end of our garden season, when we have a ton of extra cucumbers and peppers. My recipe for pickles is on page 53, but you can play around with a million different spices and vinegars to make yours unique. My favorite things to pickle are cucumbers, pepperoncini, banana peppers, hot peppers, and green beans.

Jams

I always thought making jam was a huge, convoluted process, but now I know that it couldn't be easier! Check out my any-berry jam recipe on page 242 for all of the details. And remember that jams aren't just for berries: Tomato and carrot jams are delicious and unique!

Freezing sliced veggies

This is the easiest way to store vegetables in the off-season. When we have a huge harvest and can't use it all up, I'll slice an eggplant into rounds for future Eggplant Parmesan Lasagna (page 129) or cut bell peppers into slices for a hearty Stuffed Pepper Casserole (page 229).

Place the sliced or chopped veggies in a freezer-safe container or bag and label it with the date. Use it within a year.

Freezing purees

Making purees always brings back memories of making baby food for my kids. It's so nice to have them on hand to make recipes like Carrot Ginger Soup (page 187) more quickly. Steam or boil your veggies before blending them into a puree.

Once the puree cools, place it in a freezer-safe container. I use old baby-food freezer containers, which work perfectly.

Dried spices

I use this method mainly for spices to sprinkle on recipes year-round. Place the leaves of parsley, rosemary, mint, thyme, or sage on a baking sheet and bake at 250°F for 3 to 4 hours. Once the leaves are completely dry, crumble them into tiny pieces and place them in spice jars. Enjoy your homemade dried spices for up to a year.

Canning

Canning is the one long-term storage process that I haven't played around with, since it takes a little more effort; for more info on canning, online articles and YouTube videos are great resources.

TOMATOES

Anel's

Tomato Tips

Ideal planting time

A few days to a few weeks after the last frost. When night time temperatures are consistently over 50°F, you're good to go. In New England, that generally hits around Mother's Day.

When to harvest

There are many different varieties of tomatoes, but generally when the fruit starts to turn red (or whatever color the tomatoes are supposed to be), it's ready. I like to harvest a tomato as soon as I see a little red on it. I leave it in a basket in the house to fully ripen to ensure those pesky squirrels don't eat it before we can.

1. Tomatoes love to be planted near basil (hello, Caprese salads!). Basil repels insects that might eat your tomato plants and can even improve the flavor of the fruit. There are studies proving that tomato plants grown near basil yield more fruit.

2. Prune your tomatoes, especially if they are taller than a foot. Why? Having leaves that hang down to the ground allows bugs easier access to the plant. Once the fruit begins to develop, remove the bottom leaves that have no use, allowing the plant to use more energy to develop that fruit.
Pro tip: Be sure to leave 30 percent of the plant as leaves.

3. Tomato suckers be gone! A sucker is essentially a new plant growing within the plant. You'll know you have a sucker if you see a new growth between the stem and a branch of the plant. Pinch those suckers right off or they'll draw energy away from the main plant. Fun fact: If you plant that sucker in your soil, it will grow roots and become a whole new tomato plant.

4. Tomatoes thrive in 80°F to 90°F weather but don't like extreme heat. They'll hit pause on new growth and fruit development if it's too hot.

5. At the end of the season, chop off the top of the plant to prevent new growth and give the plant time to develop its existing fruit.

 Offshoot
How to Preserve Diced Tomatoes

There are many ways to preserve and store tomatoes. You can dry them, can them, or make them into tomato sauce. My favorite method is to make a pantry staple that can be used in a million and one different ways: diced tomatoes.

The process of canning is too labor-intensive for my taste, so I freeze my diced tomatoes and defrost one of these bags every week or two in the off-season to make Nana's Tomato Sauce (page 26), Shakshuka (page 213), Vegetarian Chili (page 222), Caponata (page 117), or Creamy Dairy-Free Tomato Soup (page 46), among countless other recipes.

Makes 5 pint-sized freezer bags

11 cups Roma, plum, or heirloom tomatoes of any size and color
1 teaspoon sea salt
1 teaspoon black pepper
5 freezer bags

1. Fill a large Dutch oven or saucepan halfway with water and bring to a boil.

2. Use a knife to cut a small X in the bottom of each tomato. This is called "scoring" and will make removing the skin later much easier.

3. Gently drop the tomatoes, three to four at a time, into the boiling water and cook until the skin starts to pull away from the tomato, 1 to 2 minutes.

4. With a slotted spoon, move the tomatoes into an ice bath and remove the skin with your fingers as soon as it's cool enough to do so.

5. Dice each tomato, removing the core.

6. Repeat steps 3 to 5 until all of the tomatoes are diced.

7. Place the tomatoes in a large saucepan over medium-high heat and bring to a boil. Add salt and pepper and stir.

8. Simmer until they begin to reduce, 10 minutes, then let cool.

9. Label five freezer-safe bags with the date and place the tomatoes inside, sealing tightly. I recommend measuring out 1¾ cups of cooked tomatoes for each bag, so it equals about 14.5 ounces, the usual size of a store-bought can of diced tomatoes.

Nana's Tomato Sauce

Cross-Pollination

2 tablespoons extra virgin olive oil
1 yellow onion, chopped
5 garlic cloves, halved
One 28-ounce can crushed tomatoes
5 to 6 medium tomatoes, finely chopped
One 6-ounce can tomato paste
1 tablespoon dried oregano
1 tablespoon dried basil
1 bay leaf
Sea salt and black pepper

Growing up, we spent a lot of time with my Italian grandparents. My Nana would make her famous red sauce every Sunday without fail. When we weren't with her, my dad would make it. The smell of this sauce cooking is Sunday afternoons for me. It is so simple and clean, as the best recipes often are. Blending the sauce is optional if you don't like tomato chunks, but it's how Nana did it, and I'm a traditionalist when it comes to a family recipe.

1. Heat the olive oil in a large Dutch oven or pot over medium heat.

2. Add the onion and cook until translucent, stirring occasionally, for 7 to 10 minutes.

3. Add the garlic and cook until fragrant, stirring constantly, for 1 to 2 more minutes.

4. With a slotted spoon, remove the onions and garlic from the oil and discard them.

5. Add the crushed tomatoes, chopped tomatoes, tomato paste, oregano, basil, bay leaf, salt, and pepper, and give it a good stir.

6. Reduce the heat to low and partially cover the pot. Simmer for about 60 minutes, stirring every 10 to 15 minutes or so.

7. Remove the bay leaf. With an immersion blender, blend the sauce until mostly smooth.

Nana's Meatballs

Cross-Pollination

1 pound ground beef
1 egg
½ cup Italian bread crumbs
½ cup Parmesan, plus more for serving
1 medium yellow onion, finely chopped
3 garlic cloves, minced or pressed
1 teaspoon sea salt
½ teaspoon black pepper
½ teaspoon dried oregano
4 cups tomato sauce (see Nana's Tomato Sauce, page 26)
One 16-ounce box pasta, cooked

In addition to her famous tomato sauce (see page 26), my Nana would make meatballs every Sunday. I now make them for my kids once a week (admittedly not always on Sundays), and they gobble them up. Nana used to make half of them as outlined in this recipe and half with a handful of pine nuts and raisins mixed in, which is common in Southern Italy or Sicily.

1. Gently mix the beef, egg, bread crumbs, Parmesan, onion, garlic, salt, pepper, and oregano in a large bowl with your hands until just combined.

2. Form the mixture into 1-inch balls.

3. Pour the tomato sauce into a large Dutch oven or pot, then add the meatballs.

4. Cook the meatballs in the tomato sauce on medium-low heat for about 1 hour or until they are cooked through.

5. Serve over a bowl of pasta. Sprinkle extra Parmesan on top.

Tomato Confit

Cross-Pollination

3 cups cherry tomatoes or 10 large
   tomatoes, halved
1 head of garlic, peeled and divided into
   cloves
1½ cups extra virgin olive oil
Sea salt and black pepper
3 to 4 fresh thyme sprigs
Large handful of basil leaves

Tomato confit is one of my favorite discoveries since we started our garden. It's an easy way to use up the seemingly endless amount of cherry tomatoes we yield at the end of the season. There are countless possibilities for how to eat it. Smeared on toast? Delicious. Plopped on a bright green salad? Delectable! Served as a side dish? The perfect complement to any protein.

1. Preheat the oven to 250°F.
2. Place the tomatoes in a 9-inch square baking dish in a single layer. Place the garlic cloves between the tomatoes.
3. Pour the oil over the tomatoes. Season with salt and pepper, then top with thyme and basil.
4. Bake for 90 minutes, until the tomatoes are soft but not falling apart. Your kitchen will smell delicious! Remove the thyme and basil and discard.
5. Cool the tomatoes in their juices for about an hour, then transfer to jars.
6. Pour the oil over the tomatoes and close up the jars. Refrigerate immediately and eat within 10 days.

Panzanella

Bread & Tomato Salad

Cross-Pollination

Salad

½ loaf crusty bread (like ciabatta or
   sourdough), cut into 1-inch cubes
   (see Tip)
1 tablespoon extra virgin olive oil
1½ teaspoons sea salt, divided
4 very ripe large tomatoes, 6 small
   tomatoes, or 20 baby tomatoes
1 red onion, thinly sliced
1 cup fresh mozzarella, torn or roughly cut
1 cup basil leaves, roughly chopped, plus
   more for garnish

Dressing

¼ cup extra virgin olive oil
2 tablespoons red wine vinegar
2 garlic cloves, minced or pressed
½ teaspoon Dijon mustard
½ teaspoon sea salt
¼ teaspoon black pepper

I first fell in love with panzanella during a semester abroad in Florence, when my host mother taught me how to make it. It's a great way to use up extra tomatoes of any size or color and also gives you something to do with stale bread. What comes out of these two simple ingredients is one of the best salads you've ever tasted, though it started out as an Italian "peasant dish" made by people who needed a use for old bread that they couldn't afford to waste.

1. Preheat the oven to 400°F.

2. In a large bowl, mix the bread cubes with olive oil and 1 teaspoon of salt. Toss with tongs until the bread is nicely coated in oil.

3. Spread the bread cubes on a large baking sheet in one layer and bake for 10 to 12 minutes, until the edges are crisp and golden. Let cool for 10 minutes.

4. Meanwhile, make the dressing. Add the oil, vinegar, garlic, mustard, salt, and pepper to a mason jar. Shake well to combine. Set aside.

5. Cut the tomatoes into wedges about the same size as the bread. If you're using baby tomatoes, halve them. Place the tomatoes in a large bowl and toss with ½ teaspoon salt.

6. Add the bread, onions, mozzarella, and basil to the bowl.

7. Toss to coat with dressing, then let the salad sit for at least 20 minutes before serving. Garnish with the extra basil leaves.

Tip

If the bread is stale, even better!

My Favorite Summer Salad

Cross-Pollination

3 cups cherry or grape tomatoes, halved (I like a mix of yellow and red)

2 avocados, cubed

1 large cucumber or 3 Persian cucumbers, sliced

½ cup red onion, sliced

½ cup roughly torn fresh mozzarella, optional

Handful of basil leaves, chopped

¼ cup basil pesto (see page 143)

1 tablespoon lemon juice

Sea salt and black pepper

Whenever I'm asked to bring a dish to a BBQ or summer party, I try to bring a healthy-ish crowd-pleaser that also looks good on a family-style table. This salad is one of my go-tos, and it takes less than 10 minutes to whip together if you use store-bought pesto. It's bright, fresh, colorful, flavorful, and tastes like summer in a bowl.

1. In a large bowl, combine the tomatoes, avocados, cucumber, onion, mozzarella, if desired, and basil leaves.

2. In a small bowl, mix the pesto, lemon juice, salt, and pepper.

3. Pour the dressing over the salad and toss to combine. Serve immediately.

Tomato Caesar

Cross-Pollination

Salad

3 to 4 medium tomatoes, sliced,
    or 2 cups baby tomatoes, or a mix of
    whatever you have
¼ cup shaved Parmesan
½ cup basil leaves

Dressing

Juice of ½ lemon
¼ cup salted roasted cashews or
    grated Parmesan
2 tablespoons extra virgin olive oil
1 tablespoon apple cider vinegar
1 teaspoon Dijon mustard
½ teaspoon Worcestershire sauce
1 egg yolk
2 garlic cloves
Sea salt and black pepper

I saw this on a menu once and had to recreate it at home. Tomato Caesar takes the classic flavors of a Caesar salad and marries them to the sweetness and brightness of ripe summer tomatoes. If you want a little crunch, throw a handful of croutons into the mix.

1. Add the lemon juice, cashews, olive oil, vinegar, mustard, Worcestershire sauce, egg yolk, garlic, salt, and pepper to a blender.

2. Blend until very smooth. Add water, tablespoon by tablespoon, until it is your desired consistency. (I like to make mine fairly thick and usually end up using about 3 tablespoons.)

3. Plate the tomatoes on a large platter, then drizzle the dressing over them.

4. Top with shaved Parmesan and fresh basil leaves.

Blender Gazpacho

Cross-Pollination

2 medium cucumbers
2 pounds ripe tomatoes, roughly chopped
    (about 40 cherry tomatoes or 10 large
    Roma tomatoes)
1 orange or red bell pepper, seeded and
    roughly chopped
1 small white or yellow onion, peeled and
    roughly chopped
2 garlic cloves
2 teaspoons sea salt
Black pepper
Olive oil
2 tablespoons red wine vinegar or
    sherry vinegar
½ cup chopped chives

For Serving, optional
Diced tomatoes
Diced bell peppers

Gazpacho is the epitome of summer eating. I crave this cold, veggie-packed soup constantly in the warmer months. It's sweet, tangy, punchy, and delightfully refreshing. And it couldn't be easier to make! Throw all the ingredients in a blender and enjoy. Serve it as an appetizer in shot glasses or tiny mugs for a fun twist.

1. Dice half of one cucumber and set aside for later. Peel the remaining cucumbers.

2. Add the tomatoes, peeled cucumbers, bell pepper, onion, garlic, ½ cup water, salt, and black pepper into a blender, working in batches if necessary. Blend until very smooth.

3. Add 1 tablespoon of olive oil and vinegar and blend once more.

4. Add more salt and pepper as needed. If the mixture feels too watery, add more olive oil for creaminess.

5. Transfer to an airtight container or jar and chill for at least 2 hours before serving.

6. Serve with the reserved diced cucumber, chives, and a drizzle of olive oil. Top with diced tomatoes and bell peppers if desired.

Note

If you want some protein with this soup, add grilled shrimp on top.

Braised Tomatoes

with Burrata

Cross-Pollination

¾ cup olive oil

4 cups baby or grape tomatoes (30 to 40)

Sea salt and black pepper

6 garlic cloves, minced or pressed

6 basil leaves, roughly chopped, plus more
for serving

8 ounces burrata

Balsamic glaze, optional

Crusty bread, toasted, for serving

If you're looking for an addictive, flavorful appetizer to serve to family and friends (or just yourself), look no further. This recipe will make your kitchen smell like Italy and tickle your taste buds with bursts of brightness from the tomatoes, creaminess from the burrata, and punch from the garlic. I guarantee you'll come back for more...and more and more.

1. Heat the olive oil in a large pan over medium heat.

2. Add the tomatoes, ½ teaspoon salt, ½ teaspoon pepper, garlic, and basil, and stir to combine.

3. Cover the pan and cook until the tomatoes are blistered, about 20 minutes, stirring halfway through.

4. Preheat the oven to broil on medium-high heat.

5. Remove the lid and place the pan in the broiler until the tomatoes begin to char, 5 to 7 minutes.

6. Place the burrata in a large serving dish and sprinkle on a pinch of salt and pepper.

7. Spoon the hot tomato mixture over the cheese. Drizzle with balsamic glaze, if using, and top with more chopped basil.

8. Serve with toasted bread.

Roasted Chicken Thighs

with Tomatoes & Feta

Cross-Pollination

4 to 6 bone-in, skin-on chicken thighs
3 teaspoons sea salt, divided
1 tablespoon unsalted butter
2 cups cherry tomatoes
1 medium red onion, sliced
5 to 6 garlic cloves
2 oregano sprigs, plus more for garnish
3 tablespoons red wine vinegar

Feta Sauce

1 cup plain unsweetened Greek yogurt
½ cup crumbled or chopped feta
2 tablespoons olive oil
1 tablespoon lemon juice
Sea salt

An easy and impressive weeknight dinner that takes minimal effort but produces maximum results. It's also a great dish to serve for a dinner party, because it's easily scalable for small or large groups.

1. Preheat the oven to 450°F.

2. Pat the chicken dry with paper towels and season all over with 2 teaspoons of salt.

3. Heat the butter in a large cast-iron skillet over medium-high heat. Add the chicken, skin side down, and cook until the skin is crispy and golden, 10 to 12 minutes. Try not to move the chicken around much and don't flip it.

4. Transfer the chicken to a plate, skin side up, and set aside.

5. Add the tomatoes, onion, garlic, oregano, vinegar, and 1 teaspoon of salt to the skillet. Cook, stirring occasionally, until the onions are slightly translucent, 5 to 7 minutes.

6. Add the chicken back to the pan, skin side up, and transfer the pan to the oven. Roast for 18 to 20 minutes, until the chicken is cooked through, with an internal temperature of 165°F.

7. While the chicken is roasting, make the sauce: Mix the yogurt, feta, olive oil, 2 tablespoons water, and lemon juice. Season with salt as needed.

8. Place the chicken on a platter and top with the tomato mixture. Drizzle the sauce over everything and garnish with oregano leaves.

Mediterranean Pasta Salad

Cross-Pollination

A bright and easy pasta salad full of greens, flavor, and zest. And it takes less than half an hour to make. Want to switch it up with a different grain? Swap in quinoa, pearl couscous, farro, or orzo for the pasta.

Salad

10 ounces pasta (I like rotini or fusilli)
Olive oil
¼ cup pine nuts, toasted
2 cups cherry tomatoes, halved
1 medium cucumber, quartered lengthwise and chopped
2 cups arugula
1 cup crumbled feta
1 cup kalamata olives, halved
1 cup basil leaves, chopped or torn
½ cup mint leaves, chopped or torn
½ cup chopped sun-dried tomatoes in olive oil

Dressing

¼ cup extra virgin olive oil, plus more for drizzling
Juice of 1 lemon
2 teaspoons balsamic vinegar
1 teaspoon Dijon mustard
2 garlic cloves, minced or pressed
1 teaspoon dried parsley
Sea salt and black pepper

1. Cook your pasta in salted water according to package directions. Drain, then toss with olive oil and let cool. If you're in a time pinch, rinse with cold water to cool instead.

2. While the pasta is cooking, make the dressing. Add ¼ cup olive oil, the lemon juice, vinegar, mustard, garlic, parsley, salt, and pepper to a mason jar and shake until well mixed. Set aside.

3. Place the pine nuts in a pan over medium heat and toast until they are fragrant and lightly browned, about 2 minutes. Keep flipping them so that they don't burn.

4. Assemble the salad: Place the tomatoes, cucumbers, arugula, feta, olives, basil, mint, sun-dried tomatoes, and pine nuts in a large bowl. Add the pasta and toss to combine.

5. Dress it up: Mix in the dressing and serve cold.

Flaky
Baked Fish

with Tomatoes & Olives

Cross-Pollination

1 pound white fish filets, such as cod,
    halibut, or tilapia, about 1-inch thick
Sea salt and black pepper
1 tablespoon lemon juice
1 cup cherry or grape tomatoes, halved
⅓ cup pitted kalamata olives
1 small red onion, minced
5 garlic cloves, minced or pressed
2 tablespoons capers
1 tablespoon oregano leaves
1 tablespoon thyme leaves
¼ teaspoon red pepper flakes, optional
1 tablespoon extra virgin olive oil
5 to 6 thinly sliced lemon rounds

This dish reminds me of an early summer supper in Italy, packed full of Mediterranean flavors.

1. Preheat the oven to 425°F. Line a baking sheet with parchment paper.

2. Pat the fish dry and season with salt and pepper on both sides. Place the fish on the baking sheet, then squeeze the lemon juice onto the fish.

3. To a medium bowl, add the tomatoes, olives, onion, garlic, capers, oregano, thyme, and red pepper flakes, if using.

4. Add the olive oil and toss to combine. Sprinkle on a dash of salt and pepper and stir one more time. Pour the mixture over the fish filets, then top with lemon rounds.

5. Bake for 15 to 20 minutes, until the fish is flaky and cooked through. Serve immediately.

Creamy Dairy-Free Tomato Soup

Serves 4

Cross-Pollination

6 to 8 large tomatoes, quartered, or
    2 cups baby tomatoes, halved
2 yellow onions, quartered
6 garlic cloves, unpeeled
4 tablespoons extra virgin olive oil, divided
Sea salt and black pepper
2 medium carrots, peeled and chopped
3 cups chicken broth, veggie broth, or
    water
Two 14-ounce cans cannellini beans, rinsed
    and drained
One 14-ounce can diced tomatoes
1 tablespoon maple syrup
1 tablespoon red wine vinegar
1 teaspoon dried basil
1 teaspoon dried parsley
½ teaspoon red pepper flakes
Basil leaves
Red pepper flakes

Croutons

1 heaping cup cubed crusty bread (1-inch
    cubes)
1 tablespoon olive oil
1 teaspoon sea salt
1 teaspoon garlic powder

Tips

1. For an easier version, throw them in the air fryer at 400°F for 10 minutes, stirring halfway through.
2. I recommend a blender over an immersion blender here for a better consistency.

Warm and comforting, steaming with the delicious scent of childhood, my dairy-free version of the tomato soups of our youth is made extra creamy with white beans and olive oil. It hits the spot served with a sandwich or side salad.

1. Preheat the oven to 350°F. Line a large baking sheet with parchment paper.

2. Place the tomatoes (cut side up), onion, and garlic cloves on the baking sheet. Drizzle in 2 tablespoons of olive oil, then sprinkle with salt and black pepper.

3. Roast for 50 to 60 minutes, until the edges of the tomatoes start to shrivel up. Peel the garlic and discard the peels. Increase the oven temperature to 400°F.

4. Meanwhile, heat 2 tablespoons of olive oil in a large pot over medium heat. Add the carrots and cook, stirring occasionally, until soft, 6 to 8 minutes.

5. Stir in the roasted tomatoes, onion, garlic, broth, beans, diced tomatoes, maple syrup, vinegar, dried basil, parsley, and red pepper flakes, and simmer for at least 20 minutes or up to 1 hour, stirring occasionally. The longer you cook it, the more the flavors will develop.

6. While the soup is simmering, make the croutons. Mix the bread, olive oil, salt, and garlic powder in a medium bowl. Bake for 10 to 12 minutes, stirring at least once, until golden brown (see Tip 1).

7. Let the soup cool for a few minutes, then pour it into a blender with a few fresh basil leaves, working in batches. Blend until smooth (see Tip 2).

8. Ladle the soup into bowls, top with croutons and a basil leaf, then drizzle with olive oil and sprinkle with red pepper flakes.

Beginner's Tomato Tart

Cross-Pollination

3 to 4 medium tomatoes, thinly sliced, or
30 baby tomatoes, sliced lengthwise
into thirds, or a mix of both

½ teaspoon sea salt

All-purpose flour, for dusting

1 sheet puff pastry, thawed but still cool

3 garlic cloves, thinly sliced

¼ teaspoon black pepper

¼ teaspoon dried basil

¼ teaspoon dried oregano

Extra virgin olive oil

¼ cup chopped basil leaves

Shredded Parmesan, for serving

Fun fact: The first time I attempted to make this recipe, it looked more like a tomato swamp than a tomato tart. But I've realized after many iterations that it doesn't have to be so complicated. A simple sheet of puff pastry topped with fresh, ripe tomatoes, good olive oil, and fragrant garlic is all you need for a dish that always wows a crowd.

1. Preheat the oven to 375°F. Line a large baking sheet with parchment paper. Line a large platter with paper towels.

2. Place the tomato slices onto the paper towels. Sprinkle the salt over the tomatoes and let them sit for at least 10 minutes to remove some moisture.

3. Lightly flour a countertop or surface and unfold the puff pastry over it. Sprinkle a little more flour on top and lightly roll the pastry out with a rolling pin until it's smooth and about half the thickness that it was originally.

4. Place the puff pastry on the baking sheet and cut off any excess with kitchen scissors.

5. Score a ½-inch border around the edge of the puff pastry with a knife. Inside the border, lightly poke grooves into the pastry with a fork so that the center doesn't puff up too much.

6. Place the tomatoes on the pastry in one layer, leaving the border clear. Add the garlic slices between the tomatoes. Sprinkle black pepper, basil, and oregano on top and drizzle lightly with oil.

7. Bake for 35 to 40 minutes, until the pastry starts to turn golden brown. Remove from the oven and cool for 10 minutes before serving.

8. Drizzle with more olive oil if desired and sprinkle basil leaves and shredded Parmesan on top. Serve immediately or at room temperature.

CUCUMBERS

Anel's

Cucumber Tips

Ideal planting time

The ideal time for planting cucumbers is typically after the last frost date and when the soil has warmed up. This is usually in late May or early June in the northeast United States. However, it's important to monitor the soil temperature, which should reach around 60°F or above. You can use an inexpensive soil temperature reader to check when it's the right time to plant.

When to harvest

Harvest cucumbers frequently to encourage continuous growth. Pick them when they reach their desired size, which is typically indicated on the plant label when you buy a seed or seedling. Cucumbers ripen quickly, and leaving them on the vine for too long can result in loss of crispness and a waterier flavor.

1. Pick the right variety for your taste: You might think that a cuke is a cuke, but there are a ton of different cucumber varieties. Before planting, decide how many you'll want for pickling and how many you'll want to use in salads, if you want them to be bigger and more watery or smaller and crisper. In our garden, we plant multiple varieties for lots of uses.

2. Provide full sun and warm soil: Cucumbers thrive in full sun, so choose a location that receives at least 6 to 8 hours of direct sunlight each day. Make sure the soil is warm enough before planting. Cucumber seeds germinate best in soil that is around 70°F. The same thing goes for seedlings: Ensure that the soil is adequately warmed before transplanting them into the garden.

3. Grow them vertically: Cucumbers are vining plants that can take up a lot of space. If you want to save space in your garden, consider using a trellis, a cage, or stakes. Train the vines to grow vertically using string, twine, or vegetable clips. This helps support the plants and guide their growth upward.

4. Provide ample water: Cucumbers require consistent moisture to prevent bitterness and encourage even fruit development. Water the plants deeply but not super frequently, aiming for at least 1 inch of water per week. Adding straw or organic mulch around the plants helps retain moisture, suppress weeds, and maintain a consistent soil temperature, especially during hot summer days.

5. Pollinate: Entice pollinators to your garden, especially around cucumbers, by planting flowers like marigolds or echinacea.

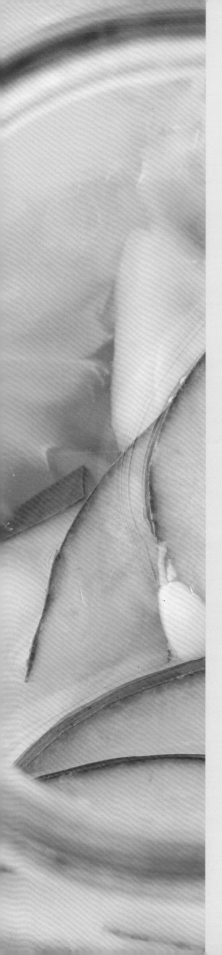

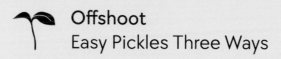

Offshoot
Easy Pickles Three Ways

The idea of making pickles intimidates a lot of people, but it's a fairly easy process with an incredibly satisfying result. I use the same basic brine recipe for all of my pickle variations, but I encourage you to play around with yours, adding different spices and flavors to customize them to your taste.

Each pickle recipe makes 2 pint-sized mason jars

Pickle Brine

1 cup white vinegar
2 tablespoons sea salt
2 tablespoons cane sugar
1 tablespoon whole black peppercorns
1 teaspoon caraway seeds

Dill Pickle

3 to 4 medium cucumbers, quartered lengthwise
6 dill sprigs
2 garlic cloves

Sweet Pickle

3 to 4 medium cucumbers, sliced into thin rounds
2 garlic cloves

Spicy Pickle

3 to 4 medium cucumbers, quartered lengthwise
1 jalapeño, quartered
½ yellow onion, thinly sliced
2 garlic cloves
1 teaspoon red pepper flakes

1. Sterilize the jars: Bring a large pot of water to a boil. Gently place the jars with their lids in the water and keep them submerged for at least 5 minutes. Remove them carefully with tongs when you're ready to use them.

2. Make the brine: In a medium saucepan over medium heat, bring 2 cups of water, the vinegar, and sugar to a boil. Reduce the heat to low and simmer for 5 minutes. Remove from the heat.

3. Let cool for 10 minutes before using.

4. Make the pickles: Place cucumbers and other ingredients in the hot mason jars. Pour the warm brine over the cucumbers until the jars are full.

5. Close the jars tightly and allow them to cool before refrigerating.

6. Let the cucumbers pickle for about 10 days. Enjoy for up to 3 months.

Hot & Cold Cucumber Salad

Cross-Pollination

Salad

6 small or 4 medium cucumbers, sliced
   into thin rounds
1 tablespoon sea salt
2 medium carrots, peeled and grated
3 scallions, chopped, white parts removed

Sauce

1 tablespoon gochujang (Korean chili
   pepper paste)
1 tablespoon minced or pressed garlic
1 tablespoon sugar or honey
1 teaspoon fish sauce
1 teaspoon peeled, minced ginger
1 teaspoon tamari or soy sauce
1 teaspoon toasted sesame oil

Inspired by the flavors of traditional Korean cucumber kimchi, this salad packs a punch with spice, umami flavors, and a touch of sweetness. It's a great side dish for a simple protein and is one of my favorite afternoon snacks.

1. Place the cucumbers in a large bowl and sprinkle with salt. Toss to coat and set aside. Let marinate for at least 10 minutes or up to 30 minutes.

2. Make the sauce: Mix the gochujang, garlic, sugar, fish sauce, ginger, tamari, and sesame oil in a small bowl.

3. Add the carrots and scallions to the bowl with the cucumbers.

4. Pour the sauce over the cucumber mixture and toss to combine.

5. Serve immediately or store in an airtight container in the refrigerator for up to a week.

Soba Noodle Salad

Cross-Pollination

One 8-ounce package soba noodles
Small handful of peanuts
1 large cucumber, diced
2 large carrots, shredded
3 scallions, chopped
Small handful of cilantro leaves
Small handful of mint leaves, torn
2 teaspoons sesame seeds
Hot sauce, optional

Sauce

½ cup almond butter
2 tablespoons tamari or soy sauce
1 tablespoon toasted sesame oil
1 teaspoon brown rice vinegar
1 teaspoon honey
Red pepper flakes

This restaurant-quality dish is covered in a flavorful sauce that always hits the spot. Add chicken, steak, shrimp, or tofu for extra protein and a more filling meal. I could eat this every day and never get sick of it.

1. Cook the soba noodles according to package instructions. Drain and rinse with cold water. Transfer to a large bowl.

2. While noodles are cooking, make the sauce: Blend the almond butter, tamari, sesame oil, vinegar, honey, red pepper flakes, and 1 tablespoon of water in a blender. Keep adding water until it reaches your desired consistency. I like it on the thicker side, so I usually end up using 2 tablespoons of water.

3. Transfer the sauce to the bowl with the noodles, add the peanuts, and mix.

4. Divide the noodles among bowls, then add the the cucumber, carrots, and scallions. Top with cilantro, mint, sesame seeds, and hot sauce, if desired.

Cucumber Basil Margarita

Cross-Pollination

1 small cucumber, diced
5 to 7 basil leaves, finely chopped, plus
    more for garnish
2 limes
3 ounces tequila or zero-proof tequila
1½ ounces agave nectar
Sea salt

This might just be the most refreshing cocktail you've ever had. It's certainly one of my favorites...both with and without the alcohol. It's light and zingy, herbaceous, and not too sweet. Try making it in large batches for an al fresco dinner party or one-off for a quiet, sunny Sunday afternoon.

1. Place the cucumbers and basil into a cocktail shaker and muddle until well combined, 1 to 2 minutes.

2. Squeeze in the juice from the limes, reserving a wedge for the rims. Add the tequila, 2 ounces of water, agave, and a handful of ice to the shaker. Shake lightly for a few seconds.

3. Rub the lime wedge around the rims of two glasses, then dip the rims into a pile of salt, spinning the rims to make sure they're all covered.

4. Add some ice to the glasses, then pour in the drink.

Papa's Marinated Cucumbers

Cross-Pollination

2 large cucumbers, thinly sliced
    into rounds
1 red onion, thinly sliced, optional
½ cup red wine vinegar
Sea salt and black pepper
Handful of ice cubes

My Italian grandfather was a quirky guy. Oh, how I miss him and his quirks. One of my favorites was his obsession with slicing his cucumbers as thinly as possible. He did his slicing slowly and deliberately, which always made the cucumbers taste better. He used to make these marinated cucumbers daily in the summer as an afternoon snack, but they're also great on top of salads and sandwiches. The ice bath makes them extra crunchy and refreshing.

1. Place the cucumbers and onion, if using, in a medium bowl and add the vinegar. Season with salt and pepper.

2. Drop in a small handful of ice cubes and cover the bowl.

3. Place in the refrigerator for 10 to 20 minutes and enjoy them ice cold!

Slightly Spicy Watermelon Cucumber Salad

Serves 6 to 8

Cross-Pollination

1 medium watermelon, cubed (about 6 cups)
2 cups baby or grape tomatoes, halved
1½ cups cubed feta
2 large cucumbers, seeded and chopped
½ cup basil pesto (see page 143)
1 jalapeño, seeded and minced, optional
Sea salt
Olive oil
Basil leaves

My dad's wife, Jennifer, makes this salad for all of her summer parties and BBQs, and it never gets old. I've taken it on as one of my own go-to salads for potlucks and backyard dinner parties, and I often end up having to send the recipe to friends and family the morning after. Because it's full of watery watermelon, I recommend mixing it up as close to your event as possible. If you're not into spice, skip the jalapeño.

1. Mix the watermelon, tomatoes, feta, cucumbers, pesto, and jalapeño, if using, in a large bowl.

2. Stir in salt and olive oil, tasting until it's right.

3. Garnish with basil leaves and enjoy!

Cucumber Mint Sorbet

Cross-Pollination

¾ cup sugar

3 medium cucumbers, peeled, halved, and seeded

¼ cup roughly chopped mint leaves, plus more for garnish

3 tablespoons fresh lemon juice

This refreshing sorbet makes the perfect palate cleanser or warm-weather dessert. It's fresh, bursting with minty cucumber flavor, and a great, easy way to use up those cukes. To make it a boozy adult treat, add 2 ounces of vodka or rum.

1. Bring the sugar and 1 cup of water to a boil in a medium saucepan. Reduce the heat to low and cook for 3 to 5 minutes, stirring occasionally, until the sugar has completely dissolved. Pour into a bowl to cool, about 10 minutes.

2. Place the cucumbers, mint leaves, and lemon juice in a blender or food processor and blend until smooth. Add the cooled syrup and continue to blend until very smooth.

3. Pour the mixture into a small cake pan and place in the freezer for 30 minutes.

4. Remove the pan from the freezer, then stir and break up the sorbet with a fork. Smooth the top before returning the pan to the freezer for another 30 minutes.

5. Repeat step 4 until completely frozen through, three to four more times.

6. Use an ice cream scoop to serve. Garnish with fresh mint leaves.

Note

If you have an ice cream maker, complete steps 1 and 2, then transfer the mixture to the ice cream maker and churn according to the instructions on the machine.

The Best Chopped Salad

Cross-Pollination

2 heads romaine lettuce, chopped

1 large cucumber, seeded and chopped

2 large tomatoes or a giant handful of baby tomatoes, chopped

One 15-ounce can chickpeas, rinsed and drained

1 cup shredded chicken, optional

½ cup mozzarella, cheddar, or Parmesan, shredded

⅓ cup pepperoncini, chopped

1 avocado, chopped

¼ cup chopped dill, optional

Dressing

¼ cup olive oil

¼ cup fresh lemon juice

1 garlic clove, minced

1 teaspoon Dijon mustard

Sea salt and black pepper

I love to eat chopped salads at restaurants, so I went on a mission to create one at home that tasted just as good, if not better, than what I'd order off a menu. The dressing is so simple and tangy, and you can use pretty much any veggies and protein that you like. I often make this as a stand-alone lunch or dinner.

1. Make the dressing: Place the olive oil, lemon juice, garlic, mustard, salt, and black pepper in a jar and shake it up. Set aside.

2. Mix the lettuce, cucumber, tomatoes, chickpeas, chicken (if using), mozzarella, and pepperoncini in a large bowl and toss with as much dressing as you like.

3. Add the avocado and gently toss once more. Top with fresh dill, if desired.

Herby Cucumber Tea Sandwiches

Cross-Pollination

6 slices white bread
2 tablespoons unsalted butter
1 medium cucumber, peeled and
thinly sliced
Sea salt and black pepper
3 tablespoons cream cheese, room
temperature (see Tip)
2 tablespoons chopped dill
1 tablespoon chopped chives
1 tablespoon chopped mint leaves

These little sandwiches are so cute and fun to serve to adults and kids alike. Save any extra herby cream cheese to schmear on a bagel the next morning. Feel free to use whatever herbs you like!

1. Place the bread slices in a line on a cutting board or counter. Spread butter on half of the bread slices.

2. Place the cucumber slices in two layers on the buttered bread slices. Sprinkle salt and pepper over the cucumbers.

3. In a medium bowl, mix the cream cheese with the dill, chives, and mint until combined.

4. Spread the herby cream cheese on the other halves of the bread slices.

5. Place the cream cheese bread slices on top of the cucumber. Cut the crusts off each sandwich, then cut into four triangles by cutting diagonally both ways.

Tip

If you use whipped cream cheese, it's easier to mix with the herbs.

Pork & Cucumber Stir-Fry

Cross-Pollination

1 large cucumber, halved lengthwise, seeded, and cut into half-moons
1 teaspoon sea salt, divided
2 tablespoons minced or grated ginger
2 tablespoons tamari or soy sauce
1 tablespoon fish sauce
1 tablespoon rice vinegar
3 garlic cloves, minced or pressed
½ teaspoon black pepper
2 tablespoons vegetable oil
1 pound ground pork
3 to 4 cups cooked white rice
2 scallions, chopped
¼ cup sesame seeds
Sriracha, optional

This simple weeknight dinner often curbs my cravings for ordering takeout. It packs a punch of flavor and works perfectly as a stand-alone meal.

1. Place the cucumber slices in a large bowl and sprinkle with ½ teaspoon of salt. Toss to coat, then set aside for about 10 minutes to draw the water out of the cucumbers. Rinse with water and pat dry.

2. In a small bowl, mix the ginger, tamari, fish sauce, vinegar, garlic, and black pepper. Set aside.

3. Season the pork lightly with ½ teaspoon of salt.

4. Heat the oil in a large skillet over medium-high heat. Add the pork and gently flatten it with a spatula so it gets a nice crisp. Cook, occasionally pressing the meat down, until the bottom is brown and crispy, 4 to 5 minutes. Flip and cook the other side until browned, 4 to 5 more minutes.

5. Break up the pork with a spatula and continue to cook until no longer pink, 1 to 2 more minutes. Pour the sauce over the pork and stir to combine. Cook, stirring constantly, for 1 minute.

6. Add the cucumbers and give it a stir. Cook until the cucumbers are nicely coated, 2 to 3 more minutes.

7. Serve over bowls of rice and garnish with scallions, sesame seeds, and sriracha if desired.

Vegetarian Rainbow Rolls

Cross-Pollination

8 sheets rice paper
1 medium carrot, peeled and thinly sliced
    into matchsticks
1 medium cucumber, seeded and thinly
    sliced into matchsticks
½ small purple cabbage, thinly sliced
½ red bell pepper, thinly sliced
½ mango, thinly sliced
1 cup roughly chopped basil leaves
1 cup roughly chopped mint leaves
Sea salt and black pepper

Dipping Sauce

½ cup smooth peanut butter
1 tablespoon sesame oil
1 tablespoon tamari or soy sauce
2 teaspoons maple syrup
1 teaspoon minced ginger
1 teaspoon rice vinegar
1 garlic clove, minced or pressed
¼ teaspoon red pepper flakes
½ teaspoon sesame seeds, optional

I was always intimidated about using rice paper to make summer rolls, but once I learned how to do it, I realized it's not hard at all, and the results are exciting and delicious. I love all of the colors and crunch in these rainbow rolls, and the fresh herbs add a little something delightful. Beware: The sauce is addictive.

1. Make the dipping sauce: Mix the peanut butter, sesame oil, tamari, maple syrup, ginger, vinegar, garlic, and red pepper flakes together in a medium bowl. Add water, tablespoon by tablespoon, if needed, to make it thin enough for dipping.

2. Transfer the sauce to a small bowl and garnish with sesame seeds if using. Set aside.

3. Place a damp cloth or towel over a cutting board.

4. Fill a shallow bowl with hot water and completely submerge one sheet of rice paper for 10 seconds to soften it. Transfer the rice paper to the cutting board.

5. Place a few pieces of carrots, cucumbers, cabbage, pepper, and mango on one side of the rice paper with 1 inch to spare. Add a small handful of basil and mint, then sprinkle with a dash of salt and pepper.

6. Fold in the sides of the rice paper then roll up from the bottom to form a tight roll.

7. Place on a serving tray. Repeat with the remaining rice paper and veggies.

8. Serve immediately with dipping sauce.

Veggie-Packed Feta Dip

Makes about 3 cups

Cross-Pollination

One 8-ounce block feta
½ cup sour cream or plain Greek yogurt
2 tablespoons extra virgin olive oil, plus
    more for serving
1 tablespoon fresh lemon juice
1 tablespoon Dijon mustard
1 teaspoon honey
1 garlic clove
½ teaspoon sea salt
½ teaspoon black pepper
1 red, orange, or yellow bell pepper,
    chopped
Half of an 8-ounce can artichoke hearts,
    drained
¼ cup chopped dill
1 small cucumber, peeled, seeded, and
    finely chopped
2 tablespoons chopped parsley
Pita, crusty bread, crackers, or
    veggie spears, for serving

I promise you that this dip will be the first thing to go at your next party. Added bonus? It's packed full of herbs and veggies. Swap my picks out for whatever you want, to use up any garden stragglers.

1. In a food processor, blend the feta, sour cream, olive oil, lemon juice, mustard, honey, garlic, salt, and pepper, until very smooth and creamy.

2. Add the bell pepper, artichoke hearts, and dill and pulse gently until mixed well but not completely smooth. The veggies should still be in small chunks.

3. Add the cucumber and gently mix in with a spoon.

4. Transfer the dip to a serving bowl and top with fresh parsley and a drizzle of olive oil.

5. Serve immediately with pita, crusty bread, crackers, or veggie spears, or store in the refrigerator in an airtight container for up to 5 days.

Easy Tuna Poke Bowl

Cross-Pollination

3 scallions, sliced, greens and whites separated
2 tablespoons tamari or soy sauce
1 teaspoon sesame oil
½ teaspoon rice vinegar
½ teaspoon maple syrup or honey
¼ teaspoon red pepper flakes
½ pound sushi-grade ahi tuna, cubed
2 tablespoons mayonnaise
2 teaspoons sriracha, plus more for drizzling
1 cup cooked white or brown rice
1 small cucumber, seeded and diced
1 avocado, sliced
1 teaspoon sesame seeds

I always thought poke bowls were only for ordering out until I made my first one. Now I'll never look back. They're fun to eat, fun to make, and can be customized in a million different ways.

1. In a medium bowl, mix the scallion whites, tamari, sesame oil, rice vinegar, maple syrup, and red pepper flakes. Add the tuna and toss to coat.

2. Cover the bowl and place in the refrigerator for 30 minutes to marinate.

3. In a small bowl, mix the mayonnaise and sriracha to make a spicy mayo. Set aside.

4. Divide the rice, tuna, cucumber, avocado, and scallion greens between bowls, then top with a dollop of the mayo, sesame seeds, and extra sriracha if desired. Enjoy it cold.

Green Cucumber Gazpacho

Cross-Pollination

2 medium cucumbers and
   1 small cucumber
1 avocado, pitted and peeled
1 yellow bell pepper, chopped
1 cup plain unsweetened Greek yogurt,
   optional
½ white or yellow onion, chopped
Juice of 1 lime
2 garlic cloves, chopped
½ jalapeño, seeded and chopped, plus
   more for serving, optional
½ cup chopped basil leaves, plus more
   for serving
½ cup chopped cilantro leaves
2 tablespoons chopped dill, plus more
   for serving
2 tablespoons extra virgin olive oil, plus
   more for drizzling
2 tablespoons apple cider vinegar
½ teaspoon honey or maple syrup
½ teaspoon sea salt
½ teaspoon black pepper

I am a classic gazpacho fan through and through, but this green cucumber version is up there with the best of them. It's creamy, herbaceous, and clean, and it hits the spot on a hot summer day. For a dairy-free version, simply swap the yogurt for a plant-based variety or eliminate it altogether.

1. Halve the medium cucumbers lengthwise, then remove the seeds.
2. Chop the small cucumber and set it aside in a small bowl.
3. Place the medium cucumbers, avocado, bell pepper, yogurt (if using), onion, lime juice, garlic, jalapeño (if using), basil, cilantro, dill, olive oil, vinegar, honey, salt, and black pepper in a blender or food processor.
4. Blend until very smooth.
5. Taste and add more salt for flavor, black pepper for spice, honey for sweetness, or herbs of your choice.
6. Transfer to an airtight container and place in the refrigerator to chill for at least an hour before serving, or up to two days.
7. Spoon into bowls and top with chopped cucumber, jalapeño, basil, dill, and a drizzle of olive oil.

LEAFY GREENS

Anel's
Leafy Green Tips

Ideal planting time

Spinach, lettuce, and kale are cool-season crops, so they're best planted in early spring or late summer for fall harvest. I usually plant seeds at the end of August for an end of September/early October spinach harvest.

When to harvest

Harvest your leafy greens from the outside in, never harvesting the full head until the end of the growing season. You can start doing this as soon as the leaves reach a mature size.

1. Plant spinach, kale, and lettuce seeds directly into the garden bed, about half an inch deep, spaced 1 to 2 inches apart. Once the seedlings are about 2 inches tall, thin them to leave 4 to 6 inches of space between each plant. Thinning spinach helps prevent overcrowding and nutrition battles between plants, and it allows for proper air circulation to prevent disease.

2. To extend your harvest, sow new spinach seeds every 2 to 3 weeks to ensure a continuous supply of fresh leaves. You're going to have a lot of success in early spring and early fall with this technique.

3. Greens can tolerate some shade, especially in hot climates, unlike most other vegetables. They like cooler temperatures, so plant them around and in between taller plants to provide shade and extend their life through the beginning of the summer.

4. Cover your kale with leaves or mulch in the fall, and it will survive the winter and pop up during the next growing season.

5. Leafy greens are very easy to grow and don't take much maintenance. If you don't have a big garden setup, you can grow them in a pot on your windowsill. I encourage every beginner gardener to start with leafy greens and herbs.

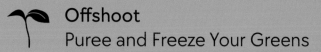

Offshoot
Puree and Freeze Your Greens

I like to use frozen spinach or kale in my morning smoothies, and I've found that the easiest way to do this with our garden greens is by pureeing the greens and storing them in closed ice cube trays or baby food containers. I learned this technique when my daughter was a baby. I would puree greens for her baby food and ended up stealing them for my smoothies!

You can use any dark leafy green like spinach, kale, or chard.

How to make pureed greens:

1. Use as much spinach, kale, or chard as you like. Wash your greens thoroughly.

2. Place the greens in a large pot of boiling water and boil just until they are bright green, 4 to 5 minutes. Don't over-boil the greens or you will lose flavor and color.

3. Drain the water from the greens. Place the greens in a blender and blend until smooth.

4. Pour the puree into ice cube trays or baby food containers. Cover and freeze until you're ready to use. They will last up to 3 months.

Use your frozen pureed greens to make:
Green smoothies or smoothie bowls
Kale pesto
Soups
Spinach artichoke dip
Green hummus
Palak paneer
Creamed spinach
Spanakopita
Frittatas

The possibilities are endless!

Kale Niçoise Salad

Cross-Pollination

3 large eggs
10 baby potatoes, washed and halved
1 cup green beans, trimmed
2 bunches lacinato kale, finely chopped
4 Persian cucumbers, sliced
Two 5-ounce cans tuna in olive oil
½ cup baby tomatoes, halved
½ cup kalamata olives, chopped
½ cup pepperoncini, chopped
¼ cup capers, drained
¼ cup basil leaves, chopped
3 to 4 anchovies, optional

Dressing

¾ cup olive oil
¼ cup fresh lemon juice
2 tablespoons Dijon mustard
1 teaspoon maple syrup
1 teaspoon sea salt
1 teaspoon black pepper
½ shallot, finely chopped

I've never met a niçoise salad that I didn't like. The key to a great one is a perfectly flavorful mix of briny pepperoncini, olives, and capers with starchy potatoes and soft-boiled eggs. You can use any lettuce you want for this salad, but we often have extra kale on hand, which adds a big jolt of nutrient-rich dark greens to a classic dish.

1. Make the dressing: Add the oil, lemon juice, mustard, syrup, salt, black pepper, and shallot to a mason jar and shake it up. I like to do this before prepping anything else to get the shallot flavor really infused in there.

2. Bring a small pot of salted water to a boil, carefully add your eggs with a spoon, and boil, uncovered, for 7 to 9 minutes. Transfer to a bowl of ice water to cool. Peel and halve the eggs. Reserve the cooking water.

3. Cook the potatoes and beans: Place the potatoes in the leftover salted water and simmer on low until fork tender, 10 to 15 minutes. Add the green beans and cook until slightly tender, 5 more minutes. Drain and let cool.

4. Place the kale on a platter and add the eggs, cucumbers, tuna, tomatoes, olives, pepperoncini, capers, and basil. I like to plate each ingredient in its own section for an impressive look.

5. Place the cooled potatoes and beans on the platter. Add the anchovies if desired. Lightly sprinkle with salt and pepper.

6. Pour the dressing over the salad and serve as is or mix up with tongs.

Cheesy Tomato Greens and Beans

Serves 4

Cross-Pollination

4 garlic cloves, minced

Olive oil

2 tablespoons tomato paste

½ teaspoon red pepper flakes, plus more for serving

1 bunch kale, chopped

One 14-ounce can crushed tomatoes

Sea salt and black pepper

Two 15-ounce cans cannellini beans, rinsed and drained

1 cup shredded mozzarella

Grated Parmesan and toasted bread, for serving

I love a vegetarian dinner that fills you up, and this recipe, inspired by one of my favorites from **Bon Appétit**, will give you just that. It's one of those dishes that you can eat every week without getting sick of it. This cheesy, hearty dish works as a sandwich or on its own and makes great leftovers, too.

1. Heat 3 tablespooons of olive oil in an ovenproof skillet over medium heat. Add the garlic and cook until fragrant, 1 to 2 minutes, stirring constantly to avoid burning.

2. Add the tomato paste and red pepper flakes. Stir and cook until the paste darkens, about 2 minutes. Add the kale and toss to coat. Cook until the kale turns bright green, stirring occasionally for 5 to 6 minutes.

3. Add the tomatoes and cook for 5 more minutes, stirring occasionally. Add salt and pepper to taste, stir, then add the beans and ¼ cup of water.

4. Bring to a simmer and cook until it begins to reduce, another 5 minutes.

5. Turn on the broiler. Sprinkle the top with mozzarella and transfer the skillet to the oven. Broil the beans until the cheese is melted and slightly browned, about 2 minutes.

6. Top with Parmesan, more olive oil, and more red pepper flakes. Serve with yummy bread for dipping.

Kid-Friendly Spinach Muffins

2 cups rolled oats or oat flour
¼ cup sugar
2 teaspoons baking powder
1 teaspoon ground cinnamon
1 teaspoon sea salt
½ teaspoon baking soda
2 large ripe bananas, peeled and halved
2 cups packed baby spinach leaves
½ cup milk (I use almond or oat milk)
¼ cup unsalted butter or coconut oil
2 eggs
1 teaspoon vanilla extract
Butter, for serving

I make these super easy, mean green spinach blender muffins weekly for my kids. They eat them for breakfast and snacks thinking they're a treat, and they have no idea how packed they are with nutrients. I also enjoy them toasted with a little butter with my morning tea. You can sub in whatever flour you prefer, but I like the texture that comes from blending my own oat flour out of rolled oats.

1. Preheat the oven to 375°F. Line a muffin pan with liners.

2. If using oats, make them into oat flour by placing them in a blender and blending until you have a floury texture. Transfer to a large bowl.

3. Add the sugar, baking powder, cinnamon, salt, and baking soda to the bowl.

4. Add the bananas, spinach, milk, and butter to the blender and blend until smooth. Add the eggs and vanilla and blend until just combined.

5. Pour the wet ingredients into the bowl and combine until lump-free.

6. Pour the batter into the muffin cups and fill about halfway.

7. Bake for 21 to 24 minutes, until a fork comes out clean.

8. Cool for 10 minutes before enjoying them on their own or with a slab of butter.

Note

Add 2 tablespoons of ground flaxseed and/or 2 tablespoons of chia seeds for extra nutrients and get creative with stir-ins. Try walnuts, chocolate chips, or blueberries.

Daily Breakfast Smoothie

Cross-Pollination

1 cup milk (I opt for oat milk)
1 cup fresh spinach
½ frozen banana (see Tip)
½ cup frozen berries (I use a mix of
    blueberries, raspberries, and
    strawberries)
1 tablespoon chia seeds
1 tablespoon almond butter
1 scoop protein powder, optional

I'm a creature of habit when it comes to breakfast, and I've been making some variation of this smoothie for over a decade. Depending on my mood and what I have on hand, I'll swap out different types of berries and sometimes even use cherries for a sweeter version.

Add the ingredients to a blender and blend until smooth. Add more milk as needed.

Tip

I keep halved frozen bananas in an airtight container in my freezer at all times for easy access.

My Go-To Massaged Kale Salad

Serves 2 to 4

Cross-Pollination

1 large bunch kale, stems removed, chopped (see Tip)
1 teaspoon sea salt
½ green apple, chopped
½ red onion, finely chopped
⅓ cup dried cranberries
¼ cup sunflower seeds
½ cup crumbled goat cheese

Dressing

1 small shallot, peeled and finely chopped
⅓ cup extra virgin olive oil
¼ cup apple cider vinegar
2 teaspoons Dijon mustard
1 teaspoon maple syrup
½ teaspoon sea salt
½ teaspoon black pepper

I've been making this salad exactly the same way for 15 years, and somehow it never gets old! The mix of the tart apple with the creamy, punchy goat cheese is what really does it for me. I serve this as a side salad at least once a week for dinner and often make it as a lunch topped with an egg or any leftover protein.

1. Make the dressing: Add the shallot, oil, vinegar, mustard, syrup, salt, and pepper to a sealed jar and shake. Set aside.

2. Place the kale and salt in a large bowl and massage the salt into the kale with clean hands until the leaves are soft and broken down, about 2 minutes.

3. Stir in the apple, onion, cranberries, and sunflower seeds, then pour in the dressing and toss. Add the cheese and toss gently one last time.

Tip

To remove the kale stems, pull the leaves off of the stems from bottom to top. Then thoroughly wash the leaves and chop them into 1-inch pieces.

Air Fryer Kale Chips

with Greek Yogurt Dip

Cross-Pollination

1 large bunch kale, rinsed, stemmed, and
ripped into bite-size pieces
1 tablespoon olive oil
½ teaspoon sea salt
¼ teaspoon black pepper

Greek Yogurt Dip

1 cup plain Greek yogurt
¼ cup chopped dill
2 tablespoons chopped chives, plus more
for serving
½ teaspoon garlic powder
½ teaspoon onion powder
¼ teaspoon sea salt
¼ teaspoon black pepper

When you taste these chips, you won't believe they're kale.
It's one of those healthy snacks that once you start eating,
it's almost impossible to stop. Plus, you'll get your daily dose
of greens!

1. Dry the kale as much as possible. Moisture will make the chips
    less crispy.

2. Place the kale in a large bowl with the olive oil, salt, and pepper.
    Toss to coat.

3. Place the kale in the air fryer basket in a single layer. Cook in
    batches if needed.

4. Air-fry until the leaves are crispy, 3 to 5 minutes, shaking halfway.

5. Make the dip: Mix the yogurt, dill, chives, garlic powder, onion
    powder, salt, and pepper together in a medium bowl. Garnish
    with more chives.

Note

The dip can be made up to two days in
advance and stored in an airtight
container in the refrigerator.

Ribollita

Cross-Pollination

⅓ cup extra virgin olive oil, plus more for drizzling

1 large onion, roughly chopped

2 medium carrots, roughly chopped

2 celery stalks, roughly chopped

8 garlic cloves, minced

Sea salt

1 small Parmesan wedge

One 28-ounce can diced tomatoes

One 14-ounce can cannellini beans

½ cup dry red wine

1 tablespoon tomato paste

1 teaspoon red pepper flakes, optional

4 cups chicken broth, veggie broth, or water

1 bunch Tuscan kale, stems removed, roughly chopped

1 loaf crusty bread, torn into 1-inch pieces

When I lived in Florence for a semester in college, my host mother would cook it for me once a week. It's a staple of the Tuscan diet, and I instantly became a huge fan. It's hearty, packed with veggies, and seemingly cures everything from a sniffle to a hangover.

1. Preheat the oven to 450°F. You'll be baking the stew after it cooks on the stove.

2. Heat the oil in a large pot or Dutch oven over medium heat. Add the onions, carrots, celery, and garlic along with some salt and cook, stirring occasionally, until vegetables are softened but not browned, 8 to 10 minutes.

3. Cut the rind off the Parmesan wedge. Add the Parmesan rind, tomatoes, beans, wine, tomato paste, and red pepper flakes, if desired, to the pot. Stir, then add the broth and bring to a simmer.

4. Kale it up: Slowly add the kale and stir to let it wilt, 3 to 5 minutes.

5. Add about one third of the bread and cook, stirring occasionally, until coated and warmed through, about 5 minutes. Taste and adjust seasoning.

6. Remove the pot from the heat. Place the remaining bread on top. Drizzle generously with olive oil.

7. Transfer the pot to the oven and bake for 10 to 15 minutes, until thick, bubbling, and golden brown on top.

8. Ladle into bowls, drizzle with olive oil, and grate lots of Parmesan on top.

Garlicky Umami Sautéed Greens

Serves 4 as a side

Cross-Pollination

¼ cup extra virgin olive oil

3 anchovies, rinsed

4 garlic cloves, thinly sliced

1 large bunch dark, sturdy greens (I prefer chard, but kale or dandelion greens also work)

1 teaspoon sea salt

1 teaspoon red pepper flakes, optional

Juice of ½ lemon

Even if you're not an anchovy fan, the flavor that comes from them breaking down with olive oil and red pepper flakes is next level for a side of greens. It is deep and rich and will make you want seconds every time. Serve them piping hot with your favorite protein. If you have leftovers, cook them into an omelet the next morning.

1. In a medium pan, heat the olive oil over medium-high heat.

2. Add the anchovies and garlic, breaking up the fish with a wooden spoon as it cooks. Cook until the garlic is fragrant, stirring constantly, about 1 minute.

3. Add the greens and cook, stirring often, until the leaves are wilted and turn bright green.

4. Season with salt and red pepper flakes if desired. Taste and adjust if needed.

5. Pour the lemon juice over the greens and serve hot.

Kale Aglio e Olio

Cross-Pollination

Sea salt and black pepper

2 large bunches kale, stems removed, chopped

One 16-ounce box spaghetti or linguine

¼ cup olive oil, plus more for drizzling

6 garlic cloves, chopped

2 anchovy filets, optional

¼ teaspoon red pepper flakes, plus more for serving

¼ cup chopped parsley

½ cup grated Parmesan

Anyone with Italian parents or grandparents knows about aglio e olio (it literally translates to garlic and oil). It's my dad's favorite pasta, and he made it every Friday night in my house growing up. It's salty and garlicky, homey and comforting. This version has all the flavors of the tasty classic dish with an extra big dose of greens.

1. Bring a large pot of salted water to a boil.

2. Add the kale and blanch until the leaves are bright green, only 1 to 2 minutes. Use tongs to transfer to a colander and set aside.

3. Keep the water boiling and add the pasta. Cook according to package directions, then drain, reserving 1 cup of pasta water.

4. Meanwhile, heat the olive oil in a large pot over medium heat. Add the garlic, anchovy (if using), and red pepper flakes and sauté, stirring constantly until fragrant and golden, about 2 minutes.

5. Add the kale to the pot and cook, stirring, until the leaves are tender, 3 to 5 more minutes. Season with salt and pepper.

6. Add the pasta and pour in half of the reserved pasta water. Cook and toss it all up, adding more pasta water as needed. (You want the liquid to lightly coat the dish.) Top with the parsley and toss lightly.

7. Serve topped with Parmesan and more red pepper flakes, if desired.

Green Fried Rice

Cross-Pollination

2 tablespoons unsalted butter, divided

3 eggs, whisked

4 to 5 scallions, thinly sliced

3 garlic cloves, minced or pressed

1 medium bunch kale or chard, ribs and
    stems removed, leaves chopped

½ cup frozen edamame

¼ cup tamari or soy sauce

2 tablespoons minced or grated ginger

1 teaspoon fish sauce

1 teaspoon toasted sesame oil

4 cups cooked white or brown rice

¼ cup chopped cilantro leaves

¼ cup sesame seeds

Any dark leafy greens work in this salty, punchy fried rice. For extra protein, add chicken, steak, tofu, or a fried egg to the mix.

1. Heat 1 tablespoon of butter in a large cast-iron skillet or nonstick pan over medium-high heat.

2. Pour in the eggs and cook, stirring frequently, until the eggs are just scrambled. Transfer to a bowl and set aside.

3. Add the remaining tablespoon of butter to the pan, then add the scallions and cook until fragrant, stirring occasionally, for 2 to 3 minutes.

4. Add the garlic and cook until fragrant, stirring for 1 more minute.

5. Add the kale and edamame and cook until the kale is wilted and bright green, 2 to 3 minutes.

6. Reduce the heat to low and add the tamari, ginger, fish sauce, and sesame oil. Give everything a big stir.

7. Add the rice and cook until heated through, stirring occasionally, 3 to 4 minutes.

8. Add the scrambled eggs back into the pan and stir it all up, breaking up the eggs with a spoon or spatula.

9. Serve immediately in bowls and garnish with cilantro leaves and sesame seeds.

Greens & Grains Bowl

Cross-Pollination

1 medium sweet potato, peeled and cut into 1-inch cubes
2 tablespoons olive oil
½ teaspoon sea salt
¼ teaspoon black pepper
2 cups chopped leafy greens, such as kale, spinach, and/or lettuce
2 cups cooked brown rice or quinoa
1 avocado, halved and cubed
1 medium carrot, peeled and sliced into thin rounds
1 small cucumber, sliced into thin rounds
1 scallion, chopped
½ cup frozen edamame, thawed
2 soft-boiled eggs, halved
White sesame seeds, optional

Tahini Sauce

½ cup tahini
¼ cup fresh lemon juice
2 tablespoons grated fresh ginger
1 tablespoon maple syrup
½ teaspoon sea salt
¼ teaspoon black pepper

This bowl is one of my favorite weekday lunches. I'll prepare the sweet potato and other veggies the night before for easy assembly, day of. If you don't want to spend time making the dressing, use pesto or whatever you have premade. For extra protein, add shredded chicken breast.

1. Preheat the oven to 400°F. Line a baking sheet with parchment paper.

2. Place the sweet potato cubes on the baking sheet. Drizzle with olive oil and sprinkle with salt and pepper.

3. Roast for 20 to 25 minutes, flipping halfway, until the potatoes are fork-tender and golden brown.

4. While the potatoes are roasting, make the sauce. Add the tahini, lemon juice, ginger, maple syrup, salt, and pepper to a small bowl and whisk with a fork. Add water, 1 tablespoon at a time, until it's pourable. (I usually end up using 2 to 3 tablespoons of water.)

5. Divide the greens and cooked rice between two bowls.

6. Top with avocado, carrot, cucumber, sweet potato, scallion, edamame, and soft-boiled eggs.

7. Drizzle the sauce over each bowl and top with sesame seeds if desired.

EGGPLANT

Eggplant Tips

Anel's

Ideal planting time

Once the danger of frost has passed and the soil temperature has warmed to 70°F or above, it's time to transplant your seedlings outdoors. Be sure to choose a sunny location. Eggplants thrive in full sun and need at least 6 to 8 hours of direct sunlight per day.

When to harvest

Generally, the fruits should be glossy and firm, and they should have reached their mature size (you'll find this info on the plant's label). Use a sharp knife or pruning shears to cut the fruit from the plant, leaving a short stem attached. Try to avoid letting your eggplants get overripe or too large, as they can become bitter and/or develop tough skin.

1. Start seeds indoors: Eggplants are warm-season plants that require a long growing season. Start the seeds indoors 6 to 8 weeks before the last frost date. Plant the seeds in seed trays or small pots using a well-draining seed-starting mix. Keep the soil moist and provide warmth and sufficient light for germination. If you can't get the seeds going in your house, buy healthy, developed seedlings.

2. Provide lots of water: Eggplants need consistent moisture, especially during hot and dry periods. Water the plants deeply, ensuring the soil is evenly moist. A drip line watering system is one of the best investments you can have in your garden. Avoid overwatering, as eggplants are prone to root rot. Applying mulch around the plants can help retain moisture and suppress weed growth.

3. Fertilize regularly: Eggplants are heavy feeders and benefit from regular fertilization. Prior to planting, incorporate compost or well-rotted manure into the soil. During the growing season, apply a balanced fertilizer (liquid for quicker absorption) every 4 to 6 weeks. This is an important part of providing nutrition for your plants.

4. Support and prune: Some eggplant varieties may benefit from staking or trellising to support their upright growth. This helps prevent the plants from bending or breaking under the weight of the fruit. Pruning may also be necessary to remove suckers and promote air circulation, which can help prevent disease. Just like tomatoes, eggplants have suckers. So pinch them off to support development of the actual eggplant.

5. Monitor pests and diseases: Eggplants are very susceptible to pests such as aphids, flea beetles, and tomato hornworms. Regularly inspect the plants for any signs of pest damage and get rid of them by either handpicking or using an organic pest control method like neem oil.

 Offshoot
How to Bread, Fry, and Freeze Eggplant for Winter

Breaded eggplant can be used in many different ways, from classic eggplant Parmesan to fried eggplant dippers. If you have extra eggplants after a big harvest, consider prepping them for future recipes in the off-season.

Prep the eggplant
1. Wash and slice your eggplants into thin ¼-inch-thick rounds.
2. Place the eggplant on a paper towel. Place another paper towel on top and press down to get as much liquid out as possible.

Bread the eggplant
1. Crack an egg into a shallow bowl and whisk to scramble. Stir in a sprinkle of sea salt.
2. Pour about 1 cup of flour onto a large plate.
3. On a second plate, pour 1 cup of bread crumbs. Mix with 1 teaspoon of sea salt.
4. Dip each eggplant round in flour, then egg, then bread crumbs.

Fry the eggplant
1. Heat ¼ cup of extra virgin olive oil in a large skillet over medium-high heat until shimmering.
2. Add a layer of eggplant. Fry on one side until golden brown, 3 to 5 minutes. Flip and repeat on the other side.
3. Place the fried eggplant on a paper towel-lined plate to cool.
4. Repeat until all of the eggplant is fried, using fresh oil for each batch.

Or bake it
1. Prep and bread the eggplant. Preheat the oven to 375°F.
2. Place the eggplant rounds in one layer on a baking sheet and drizzle with extra virgin olive oil.
3. Bake for 10 minutes, until lightly golden.
4. Flip and bake for another 10 minutes, until golden brown.
5. Let the eggplant cool to room temperature on a cooling rack.

Freeze the eggplant
Freeze your eggplant in a freezer-safe airtight container. Place parchment paper between layers so they don't stick together.

Reheat the eggplant
Place the eggplant on a baking sheet. Heat in a 375°F oven for 5 to 8 minutes on each side, until heated through.

Pasta Alla Norma

Cross-Pollination

¼ cup extra virgin olive oil
1 large eggplant, sliced into 1-inch strips
   (see Tip)
Salt and black pepper
1 yellow onion, chopped
4 garlic cloves, peeled and crushed
One 28-ounce can crushed tomatoes
1 teaspoon red pepper flakes
1 teaspoon dried oregano
One 16-ounce box pasta (I use rigatoni)
½ cup chopped parsley
¼ cup chopped basil
½ cup grated ricotta salata, plus more
   for serving

Our garden always yields more eggplant that we know what to do with! We fry it, grill it, Parm it, and everything in between. But one of my favorite ways to prepare eggplant is pasta alla Norma. This dish is almost impossible to mess up and makes for a great vegetarian meal.

1. In a large pan, heat the olive oil over medium heat. Add the eggplant in batches and cook on all sides until golden brown, 5 to 7 minutes. Transfer the eggplant to a large plate and season to taste with salt and pepper.

2. Add the onion to the pan and sauté until translucent, about 5 minutes. Add the garlic and sauté until fragrant, about 1 minute.

3. Stir in the crushed tomatoes and bring to a simmer. Add the red pepper flakes and oregano, and season with salt and pepper. Simmer until it begins to thicken, about 15 minutes, stirring occasionally.

4. While the sauce cooks, bring a large pot of salted water to a boil. Add the pasta and cook according to package instructions. Drain, reserving ¼ cup of pasta water.

5. Add the pasta, pasta water, and eggplant to the sauce and toss to coat. Add the parsley, basil, and cheese, and toss well to combine.

6. Top with more cheese and serve.

Tip

Keep the skin on for extra nutrients—
I think it tastes better, too!

Air Fryer Eggplant Chips & Dip

Cross-Pollination

Eggplant Chips

1 medium eggplant, sliced into
    ¼-inch-thick rounds
1 egg
½ teaspoon sea salt, divided
½ teaspoon black pepper, divided
½ cup all-purpose flour
2 cups bread crumbs
½ cup grated Parmesan
Olive oil spray

Dip

½ cup plain Greek yogurt or sour cream
2 tablespoons chopped dill pickles
1 tablespoon chopped dill
2 teaspoons extra virgin olive oil
1 garlic clove, pressed or minced
½ teaspoon sea salt
¼ teaspoon black pepper
2 tablespoons chopped chives

Our eggplant yield has been out of control for the last two years, and I find myself whipping up batches of eggplant chips daily in the summer. They've become a favorite snack in my house, and the dip can be served with regular potato chips as well.

1. Place the eggplant rounds on a paper towel, then cover with another paper towel to absorb moisture. Gently press down on the top towel and let sit for a few minutes.

2. In a shallow bowl, whisk the egg and season lightly with salt and pepper. To a second shallow bowl, add the flour. In a third bowl, mix the bread crumbs with Parmesan and season lightly with salt and pepper.

3. Preheat the air fryer to 400°F.

4. Dip an eggplant round into the flour, then into the egg, and finally into the bread crumbs. Make sure both sides are well coated. Repeat with the remaining eggplant slices.

5. Place one layer of eggplant rounds into the air fryer basket and avoid any overlapping. Spray lightly with olive oil spray.

6. Cook for 8 minutes, until golden brown, then flip and spray the other side. Cook for 4 to 5 more minutes, until golden brown.

7. Repeat until the eggplant is all cooked.

8. Meanwhile, make the dip. Place the yogurt, pickles, dill, oil, garlic, salt, and pepper into a blender or food processor and blend until smooth. Transfer the dip to a small serving bowl and top with chives.

9. Serve immediately!

Grilled Eggplant Steaks

Cross-Pollination

2 medium-to-large eggplants
1½ teaspoons sea salt
½ cup olive oil
1 teaspoon black pepper
1 teaspoon chili powder
1 teaspoon garlic powder
1 teaspoon onion powder
1 teaspoon paprika
¼ cup chopped parsley

If you love to grill but want a filling vegetarian dish, these eggplant steaks are hearty and bolder in flavor than you might imagine. Serve them alongside burgers and hot dogs at your next BBQ. They're delicious paired with Herby Chimichurri (page 139).

1. Preheat the grill to medium heat. Cut the green leaf off of the top of the eggplants and cut lengthwise into ½-inch-thick slices, leaving the skin on.

2. Place eggplant slices on a paper towel and sprinkle ½ teaspoon of salt on top. Place another paper towel over them to remove some of the water.

3. In a small bowl, mix the olive oil, salt, black pepper, chili powder, garlic powder, onion powder, and paprika.

4. Brush the spice mixture onto both sides of each eggplant steak. You will have extra; keep it for later.

5. Place the eggplant on the grill and cook, covered, for 5 to 6 minutes, until it starts to brown and feel tender.

6. Flip the eggplant and brush on more of the marinade. Cook, covered, for another 5 minutes on the other side until browned.

7. Transfer to a serving plate and sprinkle with parsley.

Spicy Garlicky Eggplant

Cross-Pollination

1 tablespoon olive oil
2 medium eggplants, peeled and cut into
    1-inch cubes
4 scallions, divided
3 garlic cloves, minced or pressed
1 red chile, minced
1 tablespoon minced ginger
1 tablespoon rice wine vinegar
1 tablespoon tamari or soy sauce
1½ teaspoons fish sauce
½ teaspoon sugar
3 cups cooked white rice
White sesame seeds

I love how versatile eggplant is, and this sticky, spicy dish really proves it. I serve it over rice or as a side with steak or chicken.

1. Heat the oil in a large skillet over medium-high heat and add the eggplant cubes in a single layer. Cook in batches if needed.

2. Cook for 3 minutes without stirring, then flip and cook until the skin is wrinkled, another 3 to 4 minutes.

3. Chop two of the scallions, then add them to the pan along with the garlic, chile, and ginger.

4. In a small bowl, whisk the vinegar, tamari, fish sauce, and sugar.

5. Pour the sauce over the eggplant mixture and stir to combine. Cook until the sauce is warm, 1 more minute.

6. With the two remaining scallions, separate the scallion greens from the whites and chop the greens. (Save the whites for another use.)

7. Serve over white rice and garnish with scallion greens and sesame seeds.

Caponata

Cross-Pollination

2 medium eggplants, cut into 1-inch cubes
4 tablespoons extra virgin olive oil, divided
1 teaspoon sea salt, divided
1 red bell pepper, seeded and chopped
1 medium yellow onion, chopped
Black pepper
4 garlic cloves, pressed or minced
1 tablespoon tomato paste
One 14-ounce can diced tomatoes
12 to 15 green olives, pitted and chopped
¼ cup raisins
3 tablespoons red wine vinegar
2 tablespoons capers, with their juices
1 tablespoon honey
¼ teaspoon red pepper flakes, or to taste
¼ cup chopped parsley
¼ cup basil leaves
¼ cup toasted pine nuts, optional
Crusty bread, for serving

Caponata is a bold-flavored, classic Sicilian appetizer that we ate day in and day out on my 30th birthday trip to Sicily. It's equal parts sweet, tangy, salty, and sour, and it tickles your taste buds in a new and interesting way. The flavors meld together over time, so I recommend making this a day before you plan to serve it if you have the time.

1. Preheat the oven to 425°F. Line a large baking sheet with parchment paper.

2. Place the eggplant cubes on the baking sheet. Drizzle with 2 tablespoons of olive oil and ½ teaspoon of salt. Toss to combine.

3. Roast the eggplant cubes for 30 to 35 minutes, until golden brown, stirring halfway.

4. While the eggplant cooks, heat the remaining 2 tablespoons of olive oil in a Dutch oven or large saucepan over medium heat. Add the bell pepper, onion, remaining ½ teaspoon of salt, and a dash of black pepper. Stir to combine and cook until the veggies begin to soften, 7 to 10 minutes, stirring often.

5. Add the garlic and cook until fragrant, 1 more minute, stirring constantly. Add the tomato paste and stir once more. Then add the diced tomatoes with their juices and stir to combine.

6. Reduce the heat to low and simmer for 10 minutes, stirring occasionally.

7. Add the roasted eggplant along with the olives, raisins, vinegar, capers, honey, and red pepper flakes and stir to combine. Gently stir in the fresh parsley and taste, adding more vinegar for tang, honey for sweetness, salt for flavor, or red pepper flakes for spice, as desired.

8. Transfer the caponata to a large serving bowl. Let it sit for 30 to 60 minutes at room temperature for the flavors to meld.

9. Garnish with fresh basil and pine nuts, if using, and serve with fresh, crusty bread.

Eggplant Coconut Curry

Cross-Pollination

2 medium eggplants, cut into
   1-inch cubes
4 tablespoons olive oil, divided
1 teaspoon sea salt, divided
1 medium yellow onion, chopped
1 medium shallot, diced
4 garlic cloves, minced or pressed
2 teaspoons minced fresh ginger
2 teaspoons curry powder
1 teaspoon ground coriander
½ teaspoon ground turmeric
½ teaspoon black pepper
One 14-ounce can diced tomatoes
One 14-ounce can coconut milk
4 cups cooked white basmati rice
Lime wedges
¼ cup chopped parsley leaves

If you're intimidated by cooking curry, don't be! This simple eggplant coconut curry is rich and full of intense flavor without hours of work in the kitchen. Plus most of the ingredients are pantry staples.

1. Preheat the oven to 400°F. Line a baking sheet with parchment paper.
2. Place the eggplant on the baking sheet and drizzle with 2 tablespoons of olive oil and ½ teaspoon of salt. Stir to combine.
3. Bake for 20 to 30 minutes, until the eggplant has softened.
4. While the eggplant is roasting, heat 2 tablespoons of olive oil in a large pan over medium-high heat.
5. Add the onion and shallot and cook, stirring occasionally, until translucent, 5 to 7 minutes.
6. Add the garlic and cook until fragrant, 1 more minute. Stir in the ginger, curry powder, coriander, turmeric, ½ teaspoon salt, and black pepper until well combined.
7. Add the tomatoes and coconut milk and stir once more. Bring the mixture to a simmer, then reduce the heat to low. Stir in the roasted eggplant.
8. Simmer on low for 30 to 60 minutes. The longer you cook it, the more the flavors will meld. Taste and add more salt if needed.
9. Serve in a bowl over rice with a lime wedge, topped with parsley.

Stuffed Eggplant

Cross-Pollination

2 medium eggplants
3 tablespoons olive oil, divided
1 teaspoon sea salt
1 medium yellow onion, finely chopped
3 garlic cloves, minced or pressed
1 pound ground beef
¼ teaspoon black pepper
½ cup bread crumbs, plus more
    for sprinkling
1 large egg
½ cup shredded mozzarella
½ cup basil pesto (see page 143)
½ cup tomato sauce (see page 26),
    plus more for serving
½ cup grated Parmesan

Even the eggplant-averse will go for this stuffed eggplant recipe that's baked until the cheese is melty, the flavors meld together, and the eggplant is perfectly tender.

1. Preheat the oven to 350°F. Line a baking sheet with parchment paper.

2. Halve the eggplants lengthwise and scoop out the flesh, leaving a thin layer of flesh on the skin so it doesn't fall apart as it cooks. Set the scooped-out flesh aside in a medium bowl. Place the eggplant halves on the baking sheet, scooped side up. Set aside.

3. Bring a small pot of water to a boil, then add the eggplant flesh. Cook until very soft, 10 to 12 minutes. Drain and set aside.

4. In a medium sauté pan, heat 2 tablespoons of olive oil over medium-high heat and add the onion. Cook until translucent, 5 to 7 minutes, stirring occasionally. Add the garlic and cook until fragrant, 1 more minute.

5. Add the remaining tablespoon of olive oil, ground beef, salt, and pepper and cook until the beef begins to brown slightly, 6 to 8 minutes, stirring and breaking it up constantly with a wooden spoon.

6. In a large bowl, combine the cooked eggplant, bread crumbs, and egg. Stir well. Add the beef mixture, mozzarella, and pesto and gently stir to combine.

7. Spoon the mixture into the scooped-out eggplants, dividing evenly among the four halves.

8. Drizzle tomato sauce over each eggplant and top with grated Parmesan and extra bread crumbs.

9. Bake for 40 to 50 minutes, until the bread crumbs are golden.

10. Serve hot with a side of warm tomato sauce.

Miso-Glazed Roasted Eggplant

Serves 4

Cross-Pollination

2 medium eggplants
¼ cup white miso paste
1 tablespoon sesame oil
2 garlic cloves, minced or pressed
1 tablespoon minced ginger
1 tablespoon sake
1 tablespoon sugar
2 scallions, chopped
White sesame seeds

Eggplant fans unite for this sweet and savory, caramelized, creamy, flavor-packed dish that will impress just about anyone. It comes together in just 30 minutes.

1. Preheat the oven to 400°F. Line a large baking sheet with parchment paper.

2. Trim the ends off of the eggplants and halve them lengthwise.

3. Score the white flesh into small squares with a knife so the eggplant can soak up more of the sauce.

4. In a small bowl, mix the miso paste, sesame oil, garlic, ginger, sake, and sugar until well combined.

5. Place the eggplant face up on the baking sheet and brush three-fourths of the sauce onto the eggplants. Flip the eggplants so that the skin is facing up.

6. Bake for 15 minutes, until the skin starts to shrivel up.

7. Set the oven to broil and flip the eggplant so the glazed flesh is facing up. Brush the rest of the sauce onto the eggplant and broil for 5 to 7 minutes, until the sauce is bubbling and slightly caramelized.

8. Plate the eggplant and top with chopped scallions and sesame seeds. Serve immediately.

Garden Ratatouille

Cross-Pollination

1 medium eggplant, sliced into
    thin rounds

1½ teaspoons sea salt, divided

4 tablespoons olive oil, divided, plus
    more for drizzling

2 red or yellow bell peppers, diced

1 medium yellow onion, diced

5 garlic cloves, minced or pressed

2 rosemary sprigs

2 thyme sprigs

One 14-ounce can crushed tomatoes

¼ cup chopped basil

1 teaspoon black pepper, divided

3 medium tomatoes, sliced into
    thin rounds

1 yellow squash, sliced into thin rounds

1 medium green zucchini, sliced into
    thin rounds

¾ cup shredded mozzarella or
    crumbled goat cheese, optional

½ teaspoon dried oregano

Fresh basil or thyme leaves

Yep, just like the movie! Except this version doesn't require a lot of technique. It's rustic and includes a ton of fresh veggies. Serve it as a bright and fresh side to any protein.

1. Preheat the oven to 400°F.

2. Place the eggplant rounds on a paper towel and sprinkle with ½ teaspoon of salt. Top with another paper towel and set aside for at least 10 minutes to draw moisture out of the eggplant.

3. Heat 3 tablespoons of olive oil in a large pan over medium-high heat. Add the peppers and onions and sauté, stirring occasionally, until the peppers are soft and the onions are translucent, 5 to 7 minutes.

4. Add the garlic, rosemary, and thyme, and cook until fragrant, 1 more minute.

5. Add the crushed tomatoes, basil, another ½ teaspoon of salt, and black pepper. Stir to combine, then transfer to a medium baking dish.

6. Remove rosemary and thyme sprigs from the sauce.

7. Top the sauce with the eggplant, tomatoes, squash, and zucchini, alternating vegetables to make a pattern.

8. Sprinkle with ½ teaspoon of salt and 1 tablespoon of olive oil. Add the cheese, then sprinkle with oregano.

9. Cover the dish with foil and bake for 40 to 45 minutes, until the vegetables are soft. Uncover the dish and bake for 20 more minutes until the cheese is bubbling.

10. Remove from the oven and let cool for 10 minutes. Drizzle with more olive oil and top with fresh basil and/or thyme leaves.

Crispy Eggplant Tacos

Cross-Pollination

2 medium eggplants, peeled
2 eggs
1 cup panko bread crumbs
1 tablespoon plus ½ teaspoon sea salt, divided
¼ teaspoon chili powder
¼ teaspoon ground cumin
¼ teaspoon garlic powder
1 small red onion
½ cup white wine vinegar
2 tablespoons sugar
8 small corn or flour tortillas
1 avocado, diced
Chopped cilantro

These fun-to-make and fun-to-eat tacos are a great option for Taco Tuesday and beyond. You can hardly tell that there's no meat! The meaty, crispy eggplant is balanced perfectly with pickled onions and creamy avocado. Top with hot sauce for an extra punch of spice.

1. Preheat the oven to 400°F. Line a baking sheet with parchment paper.

2. Slice the eggplant into ½-inch-thick sticks. Place the sticks on a paper towel and place another paper towel on top to soak up some of the water.

3. While the eggplant is drying, place the eggs in a shallow bowl and whisk until smooth.

4. In another shallow bowl, combine the panko, ½ teaspoon of salt, the chili powder, cumin, and garlic powder.

5. Using a fork, dip each eggplant stick into the egg and then into the panko mixture.

6. Place each stick on the baking sheet. Bake for about 15 minutes, until the breading is crispy and starting to brown.

7. While the eggplant is cooking, slice the onion, then transfer to a small bowl with ½ cup water, the vinegar, sugar, and 1 tablespoon of salt. Set aside to quickly pickle for at least 10 minutes or until you're ready to serve the tacos.

8. Place the tortillas on a hot pan until warmed through, about 2 to 3 minutes per side

9. Divide the eggplant between the tortillas, then top with avocado, pickled onions, and cilantro.

Eggplant Parmesan Lasagna

Cross-Pollination

1 medium eggplant, sliced into thin rounds
¾ cup ricotta
1 cup basil pesto (see page 143)
2 large eggs
1 teaspoon sea salt, divided
1 cup all-purpose flour
1 cup Italian-seasoned bread crumbs
½ cup olive oil, divided
One 24-ounce jar tomato sauce or 3 cups
   Nana's Tomato Sauce (page 26)
12 ounces lasagna noodles, cooked
½ cup grated mozzarella
1 cup grated Parmesan or
   Pecorino Romano

This vegetarian lasagna is my dad's signature dish; as a kid, I requested it on my birthday every single year. It is my favorite meal of all time and my ultimate comfort food. I'm so excited to be sharing this with the world. Love you, Dad!

1. Preheat the oven to 350°F.

2. Place the eggplant rounds onto a paper towel. Place another paper towel on top and gently press down to remove as much liquid as possible. Set aside.

3. Mix the ricotta and pesto in a medium bowl and set aside.

4. Crack an egg into a shallow bowl and whisk to scramble. Stir in ½ teaspoon salt.

5. Pour the flour onto a large plate. On a second plate, mix the bread crumbs with ½ teaspoon sea salt.

6. Bread each eggplant round by dipping it first in flour, then egg, then bread crumbs.

7. Heat ¼ cup olive oil in a large skillet over medium-high heat until shimmering, about 2 minutes.

8. Add the eggplant to the pan in a single layer. Fry on one side until golden brown, 3 to 5 minutes. Flip and repeat on the other side. Transfer to a paper-towel-lined plate.

9. Repeat until all of the eggplant is fried, using fresh oil for each batch.

10. In a 9×12-inch baking dish, layer the lasagna in the following order: a thick layer of tomato sauce, drizzled with olive oil, a single layer of lasagna pasta, fried eggplant covered lightly with tomato sauce and sprinkled with Parmesan, a single layer of lasagna pasta, a thick layer of the pesto-ricotta mixture, and finally a single layer of lasagna pasta.

11. Cover the top layer of pasta lightly with more tomato sauce, then sprinkle with mozzarella and Parmesan.

12. Cover with foil and bake for 30 minutes, until everything is cooked through and the cheese begins to melt. Uncover and cook for 10 to 15 more minutes, until the cheese begins to bubble.

13. Remove from the oven and let cool for 10 minutes. Serve with extra sauce and Parmesan on top.

Easy Eggplant Fritters

Cross-Pollination

2 medium eggplants, trimmed and
    halved lengthwise

¼ cup plus 2 tablespoons extra virgin
    olive oil, divided

1 teaspoon sea salt, divided

¼ teaspoon black pepper

2 cups bread crumbs

2 eggs

1 cup crumbled feta

1 tablespoon dried oregano

½ cup parsley leaves, coarsely chopped,
    plus more for garnish

2 garlic cloves, minced or pressed

Tomato sauce (see page 26)

Yogurt dip (see page 93)

My entire family is addicted to these fritters. The texture is crispy and crunchy, and the flavor is meaty and herby. Dipping them in warmed tomato sauce will have everyone licking their fingers.

1. Preheat the oven to 350°F. Line a baking sheet with parchment paper.

2. Place the eggplant halves, flesh side up, on the baking sheet and brush with 2 tablespoons olive oil. Sprinkle with ½ teaspoon of salt and the black pepper.

3. Flip the eggplant so the skin is facing up and bake for 25 to 30 minutes, until the skin is shriveled and the flesh is very tender.

4. Scoop the eggplant flesh into a large bowl. Add the bread crumbs, eggs, feta, oregano, parsley, garlic, and ½ teaspoon salt.

5. Heat ¼ cup olive oil in a large skillet over medium-high heat.

6. Place 1 tablespoon of the eggplant mixture into the hot oil and form a fritter with a spoon. Fit as many fritters as you can in the pan without them touching.

7. Fry the fritters until lightly browned on one side, 1 to 2 minutes. Flip and fry until golden brown, 1 to 2 minutes more.

8. Transfer to a paper towel–lined plate to absorb some of the excess oil.

9. Repeat until you have cooked all of the fritters. You might need to add clean oil halfway through.

10. Serve hot or warm with the dipping sauce.

HERBS

Sweet Basil Tips

Ideal planting time

If you're starting with a basil seed, it needs to be planted indoors in February or March under growing lights. Once it becomes a seedling (or if you buy it as a seedling), you can plant it 2 weeks after the last frost. The later you plant basil, the better. Soil needs to be between 50°F and 70°F for ideal planting conditions.

Be sure to plant basil seedlings 12 to 18 inches apart, because they will grow in width as the season goes on, and you don't want them to get crowded.

Pro tip: Each basil seedling comes with 4 to 5 plants. You can separate them, and each stem will become its own plant. When you're planting the seedlings, massage the roots to break them up to help them grow faster.

When to harvest

Wait until your plant is at least 6 to 8 inches tall, then cut or pinch off each leaf at the base where it meets the stem. Always harvest your basil from the top of the plant first so that new growth will fill in.

1. Basil thrives in the heat and needs at least 6 to 8 hours of full sun per day. It prefers a moist soil and doesn't like it to get dry. However, if you don't create a proper drainage system, the soil can get too wet and create root rot. You can create proper drainage in a pot by adding rocks or pebbles under the pot. If the basil is planted outside, it just needs room to breathe.

2. Toward the end of the season, a basil plant will flower, which means it is about to drop seeds and stop growing. Pinch off the flowers to ask the plant to give you more leaves in the current season. Once basil flowers, it can also change the flavor profile of the leaves, causing them to taste more bitter. So pinch those flowers as soon as you see them!

3. Harvest your basil early and often, about every week throughout the season. The more you harvest it, the bigger and bushier it will grow.

4. We often harvest so much basil that we have to store it for longer periods of time. To keep your basil fresh after harvesting and before cooking with it, wrap the stems in a paper towel and store it in an airtight container or ziplock bag in the fridge. It lasts about two weeks this way. You can also mix the leaves with olive oil and freeze until you're ready to make pesto (see page 143).

5. If you're using it raw or as a garnish, try to harvest your basil as close to eating time as possible for the strongest, best flavor.

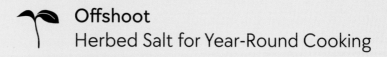

Offshoot
Herbed Salt for Year-Round Cooking

Homemade herbed salt is great for cooking, seasoning, and sprinkling. It can be used for up to a year, but after 2 to 3 months the flavor starts to diminish, so I recommend using it up quickly and giving some away as gifts.

You can use any combination of dried herbs. Our favorite ways to make this salt are air-drying and oven-drying.

Air-drying herbs:
Air-drying is the easiest method for drying herbs.

1. Tie small bundles, about 5 to 6 sprigs, of each herb together with string or twine.
2. Hang them in a cool dry place, out of direct sunlight.
3. Check on them in 10 to 14 days until they are dry and leaves easily break off of the stems.
4. Untie them over a clean work surface to catch the leaves crumbling off.
5. Remove the leaves from the stems.

Oven-drying herbs:
Oven-drying takes a few more steps but is much quicker.

1. Preheat the oven to 100°F. If your oven doesn't go that low, set it to 120°F.
2. Place the herbs on a baking sheet and place in the oven on a middle rack.
3. Dry your herbs for about an hour, flipping halfway, until they're dry and crumbly.
4. Remove the leaves from the stems.

Make the salt:
I find myself making this Italian seasoning version year after year.

1 cup sea salt
2 tablespoons dried basil, finely chopped
2 tablespoons dried oregano, finely chopped
2 tablespoons dried parsley, finely chopped

1. Mix all of the ingredients in a large bowl.
2. Pour into glass spice containers.

Garden Frittata

Cross-Pollination

8 eggs

1 cup grated Gruyère, divided, plus more for serving

4 dill sprigs, stemmed and chopped, plus more for serving

4 scallions, chopped and divided into whites and greens

½ teaspoon sea salt

Black pepper

1 tablespoon unsalted butter

1 small yellow onion, chopped

1 shallot, chopped

As chicken parents, we are always overflowing with eggs. Even after gifting some to friends and family, we have more than we know what to do with! So I make some version of this frittata weekly with fresh, bright herbs that work perfectly with the nutty, creamy flavor of Gruyère cheese. I love to pair a slice of it with a simple arugula salad for lunch or with crunchy sourdough toast for breakfast.

1. Preheat the oven to 400°F.
2. In a medium bowl, mix the eggs, ½ cup Gruyère, dill, scallion greens, salt, and pepper to taste. Whisk until combined.
3. Heat the butter in a medium oven-safe skillet over medium heat. Add the scallion whites, onion, and shallot, and cook, stirring occasionally, until soft, 5 to 7 minutes.
4. Reduce the heat to low and stir in the whisked egg mixture.
5. Cook until the edges of the frittata begin to set, about 2 minutes. Add the remaining ½ cup Gruyère.
6. Move the skillet to the oven and bake for 7 to 9 minutes, until the eggs are just set.
7. Transfer the frittata to a plate or platter immediately (it will continue to cook in the hot skillet) and cut into wedges.
8. Serve hot or room temperature topped with more grated cheese and chopped dill.

Note

Not a fan of dill? Replace it with your fresh herb of choice. Other favorites of mine are rosemary, basil, and parsley. You can also change up the cheese with whatever you prefer: Goat cheese, Parmesan, and ricotta are my other go-tos.

Herbaceous Butter Board

8 ounces salted butter, room temperature
½ cup finely chopped basil
½ cup finely chopped dill, plus more for
    garnish
¼ cup finely chopped parsley
1 tablespoon lemon zest
½ teaspoon black pepper
Finely sliced radishes, for garnish
Crusty bread and/or radishes, for serving

This trend will have a forever place in my heart. All it takes is spreading butter on—you guessed it—a board, with whatever toppings your heart desires. This version is zesty, herby, and tastes as good as it looks.

1. Spread the butter on a platter or wooden board.

2. Top with basil, dill, parsley, lemon zest, and black pepper. Garnish with sliced radishes and extra dill, if desired.

3. Serve with bread and/or radishes for dipping.

Herby Chimichurri

Cross-Pollination

1 shallot, roughly chopped
½ cup roughly chopped parsley
½ cup roughly chopped cilantro
3 garlic cloves
½ cup red wine vinegar
1 tablespoon fresh oregano leaves
1½ teaspoons sea salt
½ teaspoon black pepper
¾ cup extra virgin olive oil

Green chimichurri is a versatile condiment that comes together in 5 minutes and requires absolutely no cooking. It's delicious no matter what mix of fresh herbs you use, as long as parsley is involved. It's great on top of steak, chicken, fish, shrimp, and even eggs for breakfast. I like to keep a container of this in the fridge at all times for meal emergencies.

1. Add the shallot, parsley, cilantro, garlic, vinegar, oregano, salt, and pepper to a food processor.
2. Process until minced, but don't make it too smooth; you want some texture in there.
3. Transfer the sauce to a bowl and cover with the olive oil.
4. Let the chimichurri sit for 20 to 30 minutes then stir before serving.

Note

If you like spice, add a seeded red chile pepper to the mix.
To store, pour into an airtight container with a thin layer of olive oil on top.

Green Basil Couscous

Cross-Pollination

½ cup veggie broth or water
½ cup couscous
2 cups frozen peas
1 cup crumbled feta or goat cheese
½ cup chopped walnuts
½ cup chopped parsley
¼ cup chopped basil
¼ cup chopped mint

Dressing
½ cup olive oil
1 cup basil leaves
1 small shallot, peeled
Juice of ½ lemon
3 tablespoons white wine vinegar or
    champagne vinegar
1 tablespoon honey
1 garlic clove
Sea salt and black pepper

I've never met a green goddess dressing I didn't like. This one is top notch and just as good for dipping as it is for dressing. It's rare that both of my kids and husband all ask for seconds, but this couscous bowl always does the trick. It's tangy, savory, fresh, bright, and slightly sweet...the perfect spring dish to serve with a piece of fish or chicken. And it can stand alone for a great lunch. You can use whatever herbs you like: I tend toward parsley, mint, and basil, but fresh dill is a great addition, too.

1. In a medium saucepan, bring the broth to a boil. Remove the pan from the heat, stir in the couscous, cover, and let sit for 10 minutes. Fluff with a fork and set aside.

2. Boil a small pot of water and blanch the peas until they turn bright green, 2 minutes. Drain the peas and set aside.

3. Make the dressing: Blend the olive oil, basil, shallot, lemon juice, vinegar, honey, garlic, salt, and pepper in a blender or food processor. Taste and add more of whatever flavors you want.

4. In a large bowl, place the couscous, peas, feta, walnuts, parsley, basil, and mint, and toss in the dressing. Taste and add more salt and pepper as needed.

5. Serve warm or cold.

Note

Make extra dressing to use for salads all week long.

The Best Dairy-Free Pesto

Makes about 3 cups

Cross-Pollination

¾ cup extra virgin olive oil
¾ cup roasted, salted cashews
¼ cup toasted pine nuts
3 packed cups fresh basil leaves
Juice of 1 lemon
1 teaspoon black pepper
Sea salt
2 garlic cloves, halved
Small handful of Parmesan, optional
   (see Note)

My dairy-free pesto is what I'm most famous for in the kitchen among my family and friends. When it's basil season, I get asked to make jars for everyone I know! I make batches and batches of this deliciously tangy, nutty pesto throughout the summer and can't get enough of it. My family eats it on everything from our morning eggs to fish to pasta and as a simple dip with crackers.

1. Place the ingredients in a food processor (for the best texture) or a blender.
2. Blend well so that the texture is chunky. You want to see tiny bits and pieces of the nuts and the basil.
3. Taste and add additional salt, pepper, oil, basil, cashews, pine nuts, garlic, or lemon as needed.

Note

Obviously, as this is meant to be dairy-free. But some people like the sharp bite that comes with the cheese!

Egg Salad Toasts

Cross-Pollination

¼ cup mayonnaise
2 teaspoons Dijon mustard
2 tablespoons chopped chives, plus more
    for serving
1 tablespoon chopped dill
1 tablespoon chopped parsley
1 tablespoon finely chopped red onion
1 teaspoon apple cider vinegar
½ teaspoon sea salt
¼ teaspoon black pepper
6 hard-boiled eggs, peeled and quartered
4 slices bread of your choice, toasted
Butter
3 small cucumbers, sliced into thin rounds

We're always trying to come up with creative ways to cook the eggs we get from our chickens. This dill-forward egg salad can be served on its own, as a dip, on a sandwich, or on toast.

1. In a large bowl, mix the mayonnaise, mustard, chives, dill, parsley, onion, vinegar, salt, and pepper until combined.

2. Add the eggs and gently mash with a fork until everything is well combined and the eggs are still chunky.

3. Butter each slice of toast and cover with one layer of sliced cucumbers.

4. Top with a big spoonful of the egg salad.

5. Garnish with more chives.

Corn & Mint Salad

Serves 4

Cross-Pollination

4 ears of corn
3 medium tomatoes, cubed, or 15 baby
    tomatoes, halved
½ cup crumbled feta
2 tablespoons red wine vinegar
1 tablespoon extra virgin olive oil
1 teaspoon maple syrup
½ teaspoon sea salt
¼ teaspoon black pepper
Squeeze of fresh lime juice
½ cup roughly chopped mint
¼ cup roughly chopped cilantro

Talk about refreshing! The ultimate medley of summer ingredients comes together in this colorful salad that blends sweet, tangy, salty, and herby flavors together.

1. Cut the kernels off of the corn and place them in a large bowl with the tomatoes and feta.

2. In a small bowl, whisk the vinegar, olive oil, maple syrup, salt, pepper, and lime juice until combined.

3. Toss the corn mixture with the dressing until well combined.

4. Add the mint and cilantro and toss to combine.

Herb-Marinated Feta

Cross-Pollination

One 8-ounce feta block
2 garlic cloves, peeled
3 tablespoons chopped parsley
3 thyme sprigs
1 teaspoon dried oregano
1 teaspoon sea salt
½ teaspoon black peppercorns
Zest of 1 lemon
1 small jalapeño, thinly sliced, optional
1 cup extra virgin olive oil

For Serving

Pita bread
Crackers
Fresh raw vegetables

I based this recipe on a store-bought marinated feta that my family eats like it's our job. I use it on salads, eat it as a snack, put it on sandwiches, and use the leftover oil for dressings and marinades.

1. Slice the feta into 1-inch cubes and place them into a 16-ounce mason jar.

2. Add the garlic, parsley, thyme, oregano, salt, peppercorns, lemon zest, and jalapeño, if using.

3. Pour olive oil over the cheese and herbs until they're just covered. If 1 cup isn't enough, use as much as you need.

4. Close the jar and place it in the refrigerator for at least 8 hours or up to 48 hours to marinate.

5. When you're ready to serve, remove the jar from the refrigerator and let it sit for an hour to come to room temperature.

6. Transfer the feta mixture to a small bowl, removing the thyme and garlic.

7. Serve with pita bread, crackers, and/or fresh raw vegetables.

The Juiciest Herb-Roasted Chicken

Cross-Pollination

1 whole chicken, about 3 pounds, giblets removed
5 garlic cloves, divided
2 tablespoons olive oil
Zest of ½ lemon
1 teaspoon minced rosemary leaves, plus 2 sprigs
1 teaspoon minced thyme leaves, plus 3 sprigs
½ teaspoon onion powder
1 teaspoon sea salt
½ teaspoon black pepper
2 tablespoons butter
1 medium yellow onion, quartered
2 lemons, one quartered, one sliced into rounds
½ cup chicken broth

Every home chef has their go-to roasted chicken recipe, and this is mine. The key is lots of herbs, lots of lemon, and lots of garlic. Serve it with a side salad and don't forget to save the carcass for chicken soup!

1. Preheat the oven to 400°F.

2. Pat the chicken dry with paper towels and place it in a medium roasting pan, breast side up. Mince 2 garlic cloves.

3. In a medium bowl, mix the olive oil, lemon zest, minced garlic, minced rosemary, minced thyme, onion powder, salt, and pepper. Set aside.

4. Place the butter, quartered onion, quartered lemon, remaining garlic cloves, rosemary sprigs, and thyme sprigs into the cavity of the chicken. Tie the legs together with twine.

5. Brush the herb sauce over the outside of the chicken, getting some underneath the skin.

6. Pour the broth and ½ cup of water into the bottom of the roasting pan.

7. Place the pan in the oven and roast for about 30 minutes, until the chicken begins to brown. Remove from the oven and flip so that the chicken is breast side down.

8. Roast for about 20 minutes, until the skin on top is lightly browned. Remove from the oven and flip one more time so that the chicken is breast side up again.

9. Roast for 15 to 20 more minutes, until the skin is browned all over and the internal temperature reaches 165°F. Remove from the oven and transfer the chicken to a cutting board, draining the juices from the cavity first. Let cool enough to handle.

10. Untie the legs and remove the lemon, onion, and herbs from the cavity.

11. Place the chicken on a serving platter and top with lemon rounds.

Garden Mint Tea

1 large bunch mint leaves

One of my husband's favorite party tricks is to offer guests homemade mint tea from the garden after a dinner party. People are always impressed and excited by it. It makes a great after-meal digestive aid or refreshing addition to an afternoon snack.

1. Preheat the oven to 120°F.
2. Wash and pat the mint leaves dry.
3. Spread the mint out in a single layer on a baking sheet. Bake for 2 to 3 hours, flipping every hour or so, until the leaves are completely dry and crinkly to the touch.
4. Crumble the leaves into an airtight jar and store at room temperature.
5. To enjoy a cup of tea, place a tea strainer full of dried mint into a mug and add boiling water. Let the tea steep for 2 to 3 minutes and sip it hot. For iced tea, do the same and then let it cool.

Note

In the summer, make a pitcher of refreshing iced mint tea by placing the dried mint leaves in water and refrigerating overnight. Strain the tea the next morning and enjoy it with a slice of lemon over ice!

Garlic Rosemary White Bean Dip

Makes about 2 cups

Cross-Pollination

Extra virgin olive oil
6 garlic cloves, smashed
2 rosemary sprigs
One 15-ounce can cannellini beans,
    drained and rinsed
¼ cup grated Parmesan or Pecorino
    Romano
3 tablespoons fresh lemon juice
Sea salt and black pepper
Red pepper flakes
Bread and/or raw veggies, for dipping

I love a good dip to keep in the fridge for snacking and lunching throughout the week. This garlic rosemary white bean dip is protein-packed and full of flavor to satisfy your snacking needs. It's also nice to have on hand if friends come over and you want to serve something without a big to-do. It makes a great spread for sandwiches, too.

1. Heat ½ cup olive oil in a saucepan over medium heat. Add the garlic and rosemary and cook, stirring constantly, until the garlic is fragrant, about 2 minutes.

2. Remove from the heat and let cool for 10 minutes. Strain the oil into a small bowl and set it aside. Discard the garlic and rosemary.

3. Blend the beans, oil, cheese, and lemon juice in a blender until smooth. Season with salt and pepper.

4. Transfer to a serving bowl and drizzle some more olive oil on top. Garnish with red pepper flakes.

5. Serve with yummy bread and your favorite veggies.

ONIONS & GARLIC

Anel's
Onion & Garlic Tips

 Ideal planting time

Plant garlic in the fall for an ideal early summer harvest. Doing this allows you to harvest earlier and make room for other plants in your garden come summer. Onions can be planted with other vegetables after the last frost of the winter.

 When to harvest

Harvest garlic when the leaves are completely dried up, brown, and falling over, usually early to mid-summer if you plant them in the fall. You'll know when to harvest onions when they start shouldering. You'll be able to see at least half of the bulb sticking out of the ground when it's ready to be pulled.

1. Both garlic and onions prefer well-drained, loose soil, since they need to grow into the ground. Be sure not to pat the soil too tightly near your plants.

2. Garlic scapes are curly shoots that show up on garlic plants in late spring. A garlic scape is the beginning of the formation of a flower, which turns into a seed. Snap them off when they start to curl to stop the plant from developing flowers and focus the plant's energy into developing the garlic bulb. They taste delicious in pesto!

3. Plant onion bulbs about 1 inch deep, and if you're doing seeds, they should be sown, thinly on the soil surface, covered with soil or compost. If you're growing onions from seedlings, be sure to leave enough space (3 to 5 inches) to allow room for bulb development. It's important not to overcrowd onions. The goal is to have one large bulb instead of a lot of tiny bulbs.

4. For sweeter, smaller onions, harvest them before they start shouldering (when you can see the onion popping out of the ground). These spring onions are sweet and delicious for grilling.

5. Plant garlic in the corner or in the back of the garden, especially if you are planting in the fall. If you plant it in a primary spot, you're going to wind up with a huge hole in your garden when you harvest it in June.

 Offshoot
Drying Garlic for Year-Round Use

Our garden yields more garlic than we know what to do with during the season, so we preserve it for year-round use by drying it, which couldn't be an easier process.

Fresh garlic has a shelf life of a few months, but if you dry and properly store it, the garlic can last for up to a year.

How to dry garlic

There are two ways to do this. You can air-dry it (our preferred method) or bake it in the oven.

Air-drying (curing) garlic

1. Tie a bunch of garlic bulbs together with twine around their stems and hang the bunches in a warm, dry, ventilated space, out of direct sunlight, for up to 4 weeks. A basement, shed, or screened porch are great options. You'll know the garlic is fully cured when the outer layer is dried and crispy.

2. Trim the stems close to the base of the bulb with garden shears.

Baking garlic

1. Preheat your oven to 170°F.

2. Separate the garlic bulb into individual cloves.

3. Bake the garlic cloves for 30 minutes or until they break easily in your hands.

Storing dried garlic

Short term: Place cured bulbs in a cool, dry place. We keep ours in a small basket in our pantry, but a mesh bag also works, as the bulbs need some ventilation. Store baked cloves in an airtight container in a cool, dry place.

Long term: For storage up to a year, store in an airtight container in a cool, dry place.

Garlic powder

After the garlic is dried, simply blend peeled cloves into a powder with a food processor to use as a seasoning on meals for up to a year.

Replanting

Save the biggest bulb in the bunch for the following year's crop!

Onion Dip

Cross-Pollination

2 tablespoons unsalted butter
3 medium yellow onions, thinly sliced
1 teaspoon sea salt
1 cup sour cream
½ cup cream cheese, room temperature
1 tablespoon finely chopped parsley
1 tablespoon onion powder
1 tablespoon Worcestershire sauce
1 teaspoon garlic powder
Sea salt and black pepper
Finely chopped chives
Potato chips and/or veggie spears,
    for serving

Once you make this caramelized onion dip, I can all but guarantee you'll never go back to a store-bought version again. It is always a hit as a shared appetizer for a large group and one of my go-to Super Bowl dishes year after year.

1. In a large skillet, melt the butter over medium heat. Add the onions and salt and cook, stirring often, until golden and soft, 25 to 30 minutes. The longer you cook the onions, the more caramelized and flavorful they will be.

2. Set the onions aside to cool for 10 minutes, then transfer to a cutting board and finely chop. Set aside ¼ cup of the chopped onions for garnish.

3. In a large bowl, mix the sour cream, cream cheese, parsley, onion powder, Worcestershire sauce, and garlic powder until smooth.

4. Stir in the onions and season lightly with salt and pepper. Garnish with the reserved onions and the chopped chives.

5. Serve at room temperature with potato chips and/or sliced veggies.

Note

Make the dip ahead of time and store in the fridge, covered, for up to 3 days. For a healthier option, substitute plain Greek yogurt for the sour cream. If you're dairy-free, there are great nut-based options for cream cheese and sour cream.

White Chicken Chili

Cross-Pollination

Two 15-ounce cans white beans, rinsed
    and drained, divided
4 cups chicken broth, divided
1 tablespoon olive oil
1 medium yellow onion, diced
6 garlic cloves, minced
One 4-ounce can diced green chiles
2 cups shredded rotisserie chicken
Juice of 1 lime
1 teaspoon ground cumin
1 teaspoon chili powder
½ teaspoon dried oregano
⅓ cup chopped cilantro
Sea salt and black pepper

Toppings
Avocado slices
Shredded cheese
Sour cream
Tortilla chips
Fresh cilantro
Jalapeño slices

My (one could say *famous* in some very, very small circles) white chicken chili is my most popular, most requested, and most praised recipe. I make it every week or two in the fall and winter. It is as good on a random weeknight as it is for a dinner party. Everyone loves this soup!

1. Blend one can of beans with ½ cup of chicken broth. Set aside.

2. Heat the olive oil in a large pot or Dutch oven over medium-high heat. Add the onion and cook until translucent, stirring occasionally, about 5 minutes.

3. Add the garlic and green chiles and cook until fragrant, 1 minute.

4. Add the beans (blended and whole), the remaining broth, and the chicken, lime juice, cumin, chili powder, oregano, cilantro, salt, and pepper.

5. Simmer on low for at least 20 minutes, stirring occasionally, or until you're ready to eat. The longer you cook it, the more the flavors will blend.

6. Serve in bowls with whatever toppings you love. I take mine with avocado and tortilla chips. My husband, Anel, likes sour cream and shredded cheese, and my daughter, Amalia, likes all of the above!

Crispy Baked Onion Rings

Cross-Pollination

1 large or 2 medium white or yellow onions
¾ cup unbleached all-purpose flour, divided
Sea salt
1 large egg
½ cup milk of your choice
2 tablespoons unsalted butter, melted
2 cups bread crumbs
1 teaspoon dried parsley
½ teaspoon paprika
¼ teaspoon garlic powder
¼ teaspoon black pepper
Olive oil spray
Fresh parsley leaves, for serving

These onion rings boast a satisfying crunch that will leave you craving more... and more and more! Because they're baked and not fried, you can say goodbye to greasy fingers and hello to a tasty dish that your taste buds will thank you for. I like to serve them with ketchup, BBQ sauce, and spicy mustard.

1. Preheat the oven to 425°F. Line a baking sheet with parchment paper.
2. Slice the onion into ½-inch rounds. Gently pull each ring apart.
3. Add ¼ cup of flour and ⅛ teaspoon of salt to a small bowl.
4. In a medium bowl, whisk the egg with a fork, and add the milk, butter, ½ cup of flour, and ¼ teaspoon of salt.
5. In a medium bowl, mix the bread crumbs, parsley, paprika, garlic powder, pepper, and ⅛ teaspoon of salt.
6. Gently place each onion ring into the bowl of flour and coat thoroughly. With a fork, drop each flour-coated onion ring into the egg mixture. Coat thoroughly on all sides. Gently shake the batter off so that it's not too thick.
7. With another fork, drop the onion ring into the bread crumbs and coat thoroughly on all sides. Place the breaded onion ring on the baking sheet.
8. Repeat steps 6 and 7 with the remaining rings. Be sure to space them out so that they aren't touching on the baking sheet.
9. Lightly spray each onion ring with olive oil spray.
10. Bake for 20 to 25 minutes, flipping halfway, to brown evenly on both sides.
11. Sprinkle with a pinch of salt and top with fresh parsley before serving.

Roasted Garlic Spread

Cross-Pollination

5 to 6 heads garlic
3 to 4 thyme or rosemary sprigs, optional
1 cup extra virgin olive oil
1 teaspoon sea salt
Crusty bread, for serving

Rich, creamy, and simply divine! Versatile and easy to make, this roasted garlic spread elevates any dish it touches, but I like to eat it simply spread on crusty bread or mixed into pasta for an extra burst of roasted garlic flavor.

1. Preheat the oven to 375°F. Line a small baking dish with aluminum foil.

2. Cut ¼ inch off the top of each garlic head and place them, cut side up, in the baking dish. Place the herbs around the garlic.

3. Pour the olive oil over the garlic and tightly cover the dish with more foil.

4. Roast for 40 to 50 minutes, until the garlic is very soft and golden.

5. Remove from the oven and let rest at room temperature until the garlic is cool enough to handle.

6. Strain the oil through a mesh strainer over a small bowl and set aside. Discard the herbs.

7. Squeeze the cloves from each garlic head out of the peel and into a medium bowl.

8. Add salt and mash the garlic with a fork until it's creamy. Drizzle with a little of the reserved garlic oil. Taste and add more salt as needed.

9. Serve with crusty bread.

Crispy Garlicky Fried Rice

Crispy Garlic

1 head of garlic, roughly chopped
½ cup vegetable oil
½ teaspoon sea salt

Rice

3 tablespoons sesame oil, divided
3 eggs, whisked
2 medium yellow onions, finely chopped
6 scallions, thinly sliced, white and green
    parts separated
3 to 4 garlic cloves, minced or pressed
2 tablespoons tamari or soy sauce
1 tablespoon peeled and minced ginger
½ teaspoon black pepper
3 cups cooked white or brown rice

Elevate your fried rice game with fragrant, crispy fried garlic, which ends up being the real star of this very delicious show. This dish is a great side but can stand alone if you add a fried egg or some chicken on top.

1. Line a baking sheet with parchment paper.

2. Add the garlic and oil to a large nonstick pan or wok over medium-high heat.

3. Cook, stirring frequently, scraping the bottom of the pan to prevent any of the garlic from burning, until it turns lightly golden brown, 7 to 10 minutes.

4. Pour the garlic through a fine strainer into a medium bowl. Spread the fried garlic out in one layer on the baking sheet. Sprinkle with salt and set aside.

5. Heat 1 tablespoon of sesame oil in the same pan over medium-high heat. Pour in the eggs and cook, stirring frequently, until the eggs are just scrambled, 30 to 60 seconds. Transfer to a medium bowl and set aside.

6. Add the remaining 2 tablespoons sesame oil to the pan, then add the onion and scallion whites and cook until fragrant, stirring occasionally, for 2 to 3 minutes. Add the garlic and cook until fragrant, stirring for 1 more minute.

7. Add the tamari, ginger, and black pepper and give it a good stir. Reduce the heat to low and add the rice. Cook until heated through, stirring occasionally, 3 to 4 minutes.

8. Add the scrambled eggs back into the pan and stir it all up, breaking up the eggs with a spoon or spatula.

9. Top with crispy garlic and scallion greens. Serve immediately in bowls and garnish with scallion greens.

Lemon Garlic Sheet Pan Salmon

Cross-Pollination

1 pound baby potatoes, halved
4 small salmon filets (about 6 ounces
    each)
Sea salt and black pepper
Juice of 1 lemon
¼ cup grated Parmesan
2 tablespoons extra virgin olive oil
4 to 5 garlic cloves, minced or pressed
2 tablespoons chopped parsley, plus more
    for serving
1 lemon, thinly sliced

I make this easy weeknight dinner for my family over and over again. If you're not a fan of potatoes, serve the salmon with pesto pasta, rice, or a steamed vegetable.

1. Preheat the oven to 400°F. Line a rimmed baking sheet with parchment paper.

2. Boil a large pot of salted water. Add the potatoes and boil for about 15 minutes, or until they're easy to poke with a fork. Drain.

3. While the potatoes are boiling, mix the lemon juice, cheese, olive oil, garlic, and parsley in a small bowl. Stir to combine thoroughly.

4. Pat the salmon filets dry and season on both sides with salt and black pepper.

5. Place the salmon on the baking sheet in a single layer and add the potatoes. Brush or spoon the sauce over everything.

6. Bake for 15 to 18 minutes, until the salmon falls apart easily with a fork and the potatoes are cooked through.

7. Serve one piece of salmon with a bunch of potatoes. Garnish with additional parsley and lemon slices.

Caramelized Onion, Fig & Goat Cheese Pizza

Serves 2 to 4

Cross-Pollination

1 tablespoon olive oil
1 tablespoon unsalted butter
2 medium yellow onions, sliced (see Tip)
1 teaspoon sea salt
1 teaspoon sugar
One 12-inch store-bought pizza crust
8 ounces goat cheese
5 fresh figs, quartered
2 cups arugula, roughly torn
Balsamic glaze, optional

Savor the combination of sweet and salty in every slice of this gourmet treat. A crispy, golden crust is generously topped with velvety caramelized onions, their natural sweetness balancing perfectly with succulent figs, and then topped with creamy, tangy goat cheese. Chef's kiss to this pizza that will always leave your guests impressed.

1. Preheat the oven to 450°F.

2. Add the olive oil and butter to a large pan over medium heat until shimmering, about 2 minutes.

3. Add the onions and stir to coat with butter and oil. Sauté, stirring every few minutes, until they are a deep caramel color, 30 to 45 minutes. About halfway through, sprinkle with salt and sugar and stir to help them caramelize more quickly.

4. Place the pizza crust on a pizza stone or baking sheet.

5. Crumble the goat cheese to cover as much of the crust as possible. Place the fig pieces on and around the cheese and top with the caramelized onions.

6. Bake on the pizza stone in the oven for 10 minutes or until the cheese has melted and the crust is golden brown around the edges. Let cool for 5 to 10 minutes.

7. Top with arugula and balsamic glaze, if using, then slice.

Tip

You can make the caramelized onions up to two days in advance.

Steak & Onion Quesadillas

Cross-Pollination

2 teaspoons sea salt, divided
2 teaspoons ground cumin
1 teaspoon chili powder
1 teaspoon garlic powder
½ teaspoon black pepper
1 pound flank steak
2½ tablespoons olive oil, divided
1 medium yellow onion, thinly sliced
1 cup shredded cheddar or Jack cheese
Four 8-inch flour tortillas
½ cup roughly chopped cilantro, optional

For Serving
Guacamole
Sour cream
Salsa
Lime wedges
Hot sauce
More chopped cilantro leaves

Tender, succulent steak strips are perfectly seasoned and seared to perfection, creating the foundation for this flavor-packed weeknight dinner. Mix that with sweet sautéed onions and gooey cheese and wrap it all up in a golden tortilla for all kinds of deliciousness in each and every bite.

1. In a large bowl, mix 1 teaspoon of salt and the cumin, chili powder, garlic powder, and black pepper. Set aside.

2. Tenderize the steak by placing it on a cutting board, covering with plastic wrap, and pounding it with a meat tenderizer (or bottle of olive oil, in my case), until the meat is about ½ inch thick.

3. Slice the steak into ½-inch strips, cutting against the grain. Place the steak strips in the bowl with the spices and mix well with your hands to coat.

4. Heat 1 tablespoon of olive oil in a large skillet over medium-high heat. Add the onions and the other teaspoon of salt and cook until translucent, 5 to 7 minutes, stirring occasionally. Remove the onion from the pan with tongs and set aside.

5. Add the steak strips to the same pan with another tablespoon of olive oil and cook until pink in the center, about 2 to 3 minutes per side, flipping with tongs. Remove the steak from the pan and set aside.

6. Wipe down the pan with a paper towel and add the remaining olive oil.

7. Add a tortilla to the pan and add about ¼ cup cheese to one half of the tortilla. Add one fourth of the onions and steak strips. Sprinkle with chopped cilantro, if using, then fold the tortilla in half over the filling. Repeat to make one more quesadilla.

8. Cook until the tortillas begin to brown, 3 to 4 minutes per side. Transfer to a cutting board.

9. Repeat steps 7 and 8 to make two more quesadillas.

10. Remove from the pan and let cool for a minute. Cut into quarters and serve immediately with desired toppings.

Honey Garlic Chicken Bake

6 boneless, skinless chicken thighs
1 teaspoon sea salt, divided
½ teaspoon black pepper, divided
¼ cup all-purpose flour
1 teaspoon garlic powder
1 teaspoon paprika
1 cup honey
½ cup tamari or soy sauce
2 tablespoons apple cider vinegar
6 garlic cloves, minced or pressed
1 teaspoon red pepper flakes, optional
Sesame seeds

With its tantalizing blend of sweet and savory, this dish is sure to become a favorite in your kitchen, destined to make regular appearances on the dining table. Get ready to savor every juicy and flavorful bite of this garlicky, honey-forward chicken dinner.

1. Preheat the oven to 375°F. Line a baking sheet with parchment paper.

2. Pat the chicken thighs dry with a paper towel and sprinkle with ½ teaspoon of salt and ¼ teaspoon of pepper.

3. In a medium shallow bowl, mix the flour, garlic powder, paprika, and the remaining salt and pepper. In another medium shallow bowl, mix the honey, tamari, vinegar, garlic, and red pepper flakes, if using.

4. Dredge each chicken thigh in the flour until it's fully coated. Then, using a fork, dip each thigh in the honey sauce until it's evenly coated and transfer to the baking sheet.

5. Cover the baking sheet with foil and bake for about 30 minutes, until the chicken begins to brown.

6. Uncover and bake for another 10 to 15 minutes, until the sauce is dark and bubbly and the internal temperature reaches 165°F.

7. While the chicken is baking, transfer the remaining marinade to a small saucepan over medium heat. Add ¼ cup water and bring to a simmer.

8. Reduce the heat to medium-low and simmer until the sauce thickens, 10 to 15 minutes, stirring often.

9. Remove from the oven and pour the sauce over the chicken. Garnish with sesame seeds.

Onion Tart

Cross-Pollination

All-purpose flour
1 sheet puff pastry, thawed but still cool
2 tablespoons extra virgin olive oil
3 yellow onions, thinly sliced
½ teaspoon sea salt
¼ teaspoon black pepper
1 cup shredded Gruyère
1 tablespoon minced thyme leaves
2 tablespoons minced chives

This yummy tart features a flaky, buttery puff pastry crust topped with sweet onions, punchy Gruyère cheese, and fresh herbs. Serve it as an elegant appetizer or the star of your next brunch and prepare to fall in love.

1. Preheat the oven to 400°F. Line a large baking sheet with parchment paper.

2. Lightly flour a countertop or work surface and unfold the puff pastry over it. Sprinkle a little more flour on top and lightly roll the pastry out with a rolling pin until it's smooth and about half its original thickness.

3. Transfer to the baking sheet. Trim any excess with kitchen scissors if necessary.

4. Score a ½-inch border around the edge of the puff pastry with a knife. Inside the border, lightly poke grooves throughout the pastry with a fork so that the center doesn't puff up too much.

5. Bake for about 10 minutes, until the edges begin to turn golden brown and start to get puffy.

6. While the pastry is baking, heat the olive oil in a large skillet over medium-high heat. Add the onions, salt, and pepper. Cook until the onions begin to brown, about 10 minutes, stirring occasionally. Set aside.

7. Pull the pastry out of the oven and top with cheese, avoiding the edges. Add the onions on top, then sprinkle with thyme.

8. Transfer the tart back to the oven and bake for 8 to 10 more minutes, until the edges are golden brown and crispy.

9. Let cool for 5 to 10 minutes before serving. Garnish with chives.

Fresh Garden Salsa

Cross-Pollination

5 to 6 medium tomatoes, quartered, or 20
    to 25 baby tomatoes, halved
One 14-ounce can diced tomatoes
½ red onion, peeled and quartered
1 jalapeño, halved and seeded
2 garlic cloves, halved
Juice of 1 lime
½ cup chopped cilantro leaves
1 teaspoon sea salt
¼ teaspoon ground cumin
¼ teaspoon black pepper
⅛ teaspoon sugar
Tortilla chips

Whether you're hosting friends, looking for a quick and healthy snack, or want to add a touch of brightness to your daily meals, this mouthwatering salsa is exactly what you're looking for. It's a beautifully bright blend of garden-fresh produce with a touch of heat.

1. Place the tomatoes, onion, jalapeño, garlic, lime juice, cilantro, salt, cumin, pepper, and sugar in a food processor.
2. Pulse in one-second bursts until everything is roughly chopped.
3. Serve with tortilla chips.

Note

For spicier salsa, add more seeded jalapeños.

CARROTS

Anel's
Carrot Tips

Ideal planting time

The first seeds can be planted about 3 to 4 weeks before the last expected frost in the spring. They can also be planted in the late fall. Carrot seeds are tiny, so it's important to evenly space them out. Try to space them about an inch to an inch and a half apart. You can also mix them with sand or coffee grounds to make distribution easier if you're planting in a big area. When the seeds are in the ground, cover them with loose soil, making sure that it's airy, and organic matter on top.

When to harvest

Carrots will tell you when they're ready to come out. This is called "shouldering," because it looks like they are sticking up their shoulders to tell you they're ready to be pulled. Harvest your carrots by grasping the "shoulders" and giving it a bit of a wiggle or a twist as you pull up. If a carrot doesn't come out easily, you can loosen the soil gently with your finger and then try again.

1. Don't be alarmed if your carrots come in all shapes and sizes: long and tapered, short and stubby, thick and twisty, intertwined, and even round like a ball. I don't think I've ever seen a perfect carrot shape. Luckily, the shape doesn't affect the flavor.

2. Carrots do not grow well in very hot weather. Coolness keeps their sweetness and flavor intact. Carrots also like a hard frost (when it gets cold quickly), which makes them sweeter and tastier. In fact, I've left carrots in the ground over the winter, and they popped up in early spring. They're an easier crop because they don't have many pests or diseases.

3. Carrots love loose, deep, and well-drained soil. Before planting carrots, work the soil by removing any rocks, roots, and clumps so the carrots can grow deep. If the soil isn't loose, you may see carrots "shouldering" (when a carrot tells you it's ready to be harvested) too early and growing out of, instead of into, the ground.

4. Thinning: Once the seedlings sprout and are a few inches tall, thin them out to provide enough space for the carrots to grow. Pull out the weakest-looking seedlings, allowing the stronger ones to receive more nutrients and develop into healthy carrots.

 Offshoot
Use Carrot Greens Three Ways

Those beautiful, vibrant, leafy greens on the tops of your carrots don't have to be wasted. Their earthy flavor adds a fun twist to recipes. Blend them into a tasty pesto, add them to chimichurri, or chop them up into your favorite green salad.

1. Carrot Top Pesto

Enjoy this pesto tossed with pasta, mixed with beans, as a topper for fish or meat, a sandwich spread, or as a dip with crackers.

Makes 2 cups

2 cups carrot top greens, rinsed and stemmed
¾ cup extra virgin olive oil
1 cup spinach leaves
2 garlic cloves, halved
¾ cup roasted, salted cashews
½ cup grated Parmesan
¼ cup toasted pine nuts
Juice of ½ lemon
½ teaspoon sea salt
½ teaspoon black pepper

1. Bring a small saucepan of water to a boil and blanch the carrot tops until they turn bright green, 2 to 3 minutes. Strain, rinse with cool water, and set aside.

2. Place the olive oil in a food processor. Add the spinach, garlic, cashews, cheese, pine nuts, lemon juice, salt, and pepper and pulse in one-second intervals until it's your desired consistency. I like mine to be slightly chunky. Try the pesto and adjust to your flavor preferences.

3. Enjoy immediately or store in an airtight container in the fridge for up to a week.

2. Carrot Top Chimichurri

Add the carrot greens to Herby Chimichurri (page 139) for a fresh, earthy flavor. Serve this over steak, chicken, fish, or your favorite protein.

3. Carrot Top Salad

Add roughly chopped carrot greens to your favorite green salad, like My Go-To Massaged Kale Salad on page 90.

Carrot Ginger Soup

Serves 4

Cross-Pollination

6 large carrots or 10 medium carrots (about 2 pounds), peeled and cut into 1-inch-thick rounds

1 medium yellow onion, cut into large chunks

3 tablespoons extra virgin olive oil, divided

1 teaspoon sea salt, divided, plus more to taste

4 garlic cloves, minced or pressed

2 teaspoons grated ginger

½ teaspoon black pepper, plus more to taste

½ teaspoon ground cumin

4 cups chicken broth, veggie broth, or water

2 tablespoons unsalted butter

1 teaspoon lemon juice

Crusty bread, for serving

This velvety, creamy (yet dairy-free!) carrot ginger soup is warm, comforting, bright, and healthy. It hits the spot on a cozy night or when you're craving a double dose of veggies.

1. Preheat the oven to 400°F. Line a large baking sheet with parchment paper.

2. Place the carrots and onion on the baking sheet.

3. Add 2 tablespoons of olive oil and ½ teaspoon of salt and toss until the carrots are lightly coated.

4. Roast the carrots and onions for 30 to 35 minutes, until you can easily pierce through them with a fork.

5. Once they're cooked, heat the remaining tablespoon of olive oil in a large pot or Dutch oven over medium heat. Add the garlic and cook until fragrant, 1 minute.

6. Add the ginger, black pepper, cumin, and ½ teaspoon of salt and stir to combine. Pour in the broth and 1 cup water and stir again.

7. Add the carrots and onions and turn the heat to high. Bring the soup to a boil, then reduce the heat to low and simmer, uncovered, for 15 to 20 minutes, stirring occasionally.

8. Transfer the hot soup to a blender, in batches if necessary. Add the butter and lemon juice. Blend until very smooth. Add more salt and pepper to taste.

9. Serve hot with a slice of crusty bread.

Carrot "Hot Dogs"

Cross-Pollination

4 medium carrots, peeled
2 teaspoon sea salt
1 cup vegetable or chicken broth
½ cup apple cider vinegar
½ cup tamari or soy sauce
2 tablespoons ketchup
1 tablespoon Dijon mustard
1 tablespoon maple syrup
1 teaspoon garlic powder
1 teaspoon paprika
¼ teaspoon black pepper
4 hot dog buns

Toppings
Ketchup
Mustard
Relish
Diced onions
Coleslaw
Sliced jalapeños
Pickles (see page 53)

If you told me that I could make a carrot taste like a hot dog before making this recipe, I would never have believed you. You'll just have to trust me that these are incredible. As in I choose these over meat on the regular. The smoky-sweet marinade somehow mimics hot dog flavor but with all clean ingredients.

1. Bring a large pot of water to a boil. Add the carrots and salt and cook until just fork-tender, about 10 minutes.

2. While the carrots are cooking, mix the broth, vinegar, tamari, ketchup, mustard, maple syrup, garlic powder, paprika, and pepper in a large bowl until well combined. Transfer the marinade to a rectangular container.

3. Use tongs to transfer the carrots directly into the marinade. Cover the container and transfer to the refrigerator to marinate for at least 4 hours and up to 12 hours.

4. When you're ready to serve, place the carrots on the grill (or a grill pan on the stove over medium-high heat) and cook until they're warmed through and you get grill marks, 2 to 3 minutes per side.

5. Serve in hot dog buns with your favorite toppings. (You may have to cut the ends so that they fit into the bun.)

Carrot Hummus

Cross-Pollination

5 to 6 medium carrots, peeled and cut
    into 2-inch pieces
3 garlic cloves, peeled
Extra virgin olive oil
½ teaspoon ground cumin
¼ teaspoon paprika
1 teaspoon sea salt, divided
1 teaspoon black pepper, divided
2 tablespoons tahini
Juice of 1 lemon
1 cup canned chickpeas, rinsed and
    drained
Bread, crackers, pita chips, or sliced
    veggies, for dipping

This hummus is addictive with a capital A, and it only takes a few minutes of prep once you roast the carrots. The sweet and smoky carrots are blended with classic hummus ingredients—chickpeas, lemon, tahini, and garlic—to make a dip you'll come back to over and over again.

1. Preheat the oven to 400°F. Line a baking sheet with parchment paper.

2. Place the carrots and garlic onto the baking sheet. Drizzle with 2 tablespoons of olive oil and sprinkle with cumin, paprika, and ½ teaspoon each of salt and pepper. Toss to combine.

3. Roast for 25 to 30 minutes, until the carrots are tender, flipping halfway.

4. While the carrots are roasting, add the tahini, 3 tablespoons of olive oil, the lemon juice, ¼ cup of water, and ½ teaspoon each of salt and pepper in a food processor.

5. Place the roasted carrots and garlic and the chickpeas over the tahini mixture, and pulse until creamy, stopping a few times to scrape down the sides. Add more water as needed for a creamy consistency.

6. Taste and add more salt, pepper, lemon juice, or tahini to achieve your desired flavor. Transfer to a serving bowl and drizzle with olive oil.

Carrot Margarita

4 ounces fresh carrot juice
2 ounces Blanco tequila
1 ounce fresh orange juice
½ ounce Cointreau
Squeeze of fresh lime juice
Ice
Lime wedges
Sea salt

I have an unexpected affinity for carrot juice, which started during my pregnancies, so I gave this recipe a try, half as a joke, and ended up really liking it. I know it's bizarre, but you just have to trust me on this. Drinking a carrot margarita feels like you're doing something healthy while also imbibing tequila. As if they cancel each other out (they don't). For a mocktail version, replace the tequila with a zero-proof version or leave it out altogether.

1. Add the carrot juice, tequila, orange juice, Cointreau, and lime juice into a cocktail shaker with ice. Shake until combined.

2. Rub a lime wedge around the rim of a glass then dip the rim into a pile of salt, spinning it to make sure it's all covered.

3. Pour the chilled cocktail over ice. Garnish with a lime wedge.

Creamy Carrot Colada Smoothie

1 cup milk of your choice (I prefer oat)
2 medium carrots, peeled and chopped
2 tablespoons unsweetened coconut
   flakes
¼ cup frozen pineapple chunks
½ teaspoon grated or chopped ginger
¼ cup unsalted cashews

I love a good smoothie but get sick of
using the same ingredients over and over.
My creamy carrot and coconut smoothie
is a little different but oh so tasty. It really
highlights the flavor and sweetness of the
carrots in a creative way. The blended
cashews make it decadent and creamy. If
you want something a little lighter, swap
out the milk for coconut water.

Add the ingredients to a blender and blend until
smooth. Add more milk as needed.

Carrot Cake Muffins

1½ cups whole wheat or all-purpose flour

2 teaspoons ground cinnamon

1 teaspoon baking powder

½ teaspoon baking soda

¼ teaspoon ground nutmeg

¼ teaspoon sea salt

½ cup maple syrup

⅓ cup unsalted butter or coconut oil, at room temperature

1 ripe banana, mashed

1 large egg

1 teaspoon vanilla extract

3 medium carrots, grated

My kids love these carrot-packed muffins just as much as I do, and I feel good about serving them for breakfast or a snack. For an extra delicious treat, cut a muffin in half, place it on a griddle or pan and smear with butter.

1. Preheat the oven to 350°F. Line a muffin pan with cupcake liners.
2. In a medium bowl, mix the flour, cinnamon, baking powder, baking soda, nutmeg, and salt.
3. In a large bowl, mix the maple syrup, butter, banana, egg, and vanilla, and combine until smooth.
4. Add the dry ingredients to the wet mix and stir until smooth. Stir in the grated carrots with a spoon.
5. Fill the muffin cups three-fourths of the way to the top.
6. Bake for 15 to 18 minutes, until a fork comes out clean. Cool for a few minutes before serving.

Note

Use a food processor for the carrots instead of a grater to make the process a lot quicker and easier. If you want to add mix-ins, try raisins, coconut flakes, walnuts, or chocolate chips.

Vegan Carrot Lox

Cross-Pollination

3 tablespoons extra virgin olive oil
2 tablespoons capers with their juices,
   plus more for serving
1 tablespoon apple cider vinegar
1 tablespoon chopped dill
1 teaspoon tamari or soy sauce
1 teaspoon garlic powder
1 teaspoon onion powder
1 teaspoon lemon juice
½ teaspoon black pepper
3 large carrots
1 teaspoon sea salt

I don't like to play favorites, but this is up there as one of the best in this book! This plant-based alternative to traditional salmon lox brings you the flavors and texture you love without any of the fishiness. It's almost as good as the real thing, and when served with a bagel and all the fixin's, you can't even tell the difference.

1. In a medium bowl or container, mix the olive oil, capers, vinegar, dill, tamari, garlic powder, onion powder, lemon juice, and black pepper. Set aside.

2. Bring a large pot of water to a boil.

3. Peel the carrots into long ribbons, pressing down with the peeler to make them as thick as possible. Compost the outer skin.

4. Place the carrot ribbons and salt into the boiling water. Boil until the carrots are tender but not mushy, 1 to 2 minutes.

5. Use tongs to transfer the carrots directly into the marinade. Cover the bowl and transfer to the refrigerator to marinate for at least 30 minutes and up to 24 hours, then serve (see Note).

Note

I love to eat carrot lox on a toasted bagel with cream cheese, sliced onions, sliced tomatoes, and the marinated capers. Garnish with fresh dill for a nice touch. This lox is also great on a salad or sandwich.

Maple-Roasted Carrots

with Tahini Drizzle

Cross-Pollination

6 to 8 medium carrots, peeled and cut into 1½-inch pieces
3 tablespoons olive oil
1 teaspoon ground cinnamon
1 teaspoon sea salt
½ teaspoon ground ginger
½ teaspoon black pepper
⅛ teaspoon ground nutmeg
¼ cup chopped parsley, plus more for serving

Sauce

¼ cup tahini
1 tablespoon maple syrup
½ teaspoon apple cider vinegar
¼ teaspoon ground cinnamon
⅛ teaspoon ground ginger
½ teaspoon sea salt

This colorful, creamy, homey, rich, and root-y side dish made with roasted carrots and a decadent cinnamon-tahini drizzle is everything. I could drink this sauce for breakfast, lunch, and dinner. Sub in any root vegetables you have on hand: Sweet potatoes, potatoes, turnips, parsnips, or any combination would be delectable.

1. Preheat the oven to 375°F. Line a baking sheet with parchment paper.

2. Add the carrots to a large bowl.

3. In a small bowl, whisk the olive oil, cinnamon, salt, ginger, black pepper, nutmeg, and parsley. Pour the mixture over the carrots and toss to coat.

4. Place the carrots onto the baking sheet and roast for 30 to 40 minutes, until a fork can easily pierce them.

5. Meanwhile, make the sauce. Add the tahini, maple syrup, vinegar, cinnamon, ginger, salt, and ½ cup water to a mason jar and shake until smooth.

6. Drizzle the carrots with the tahini sauce and garnish with more chopped parsley.

Deconstructed Spring Roll Salad

Serves 4 as a side and
2 as a main

Cross-Pollination

1½ cups purple cabbage, chopped
1 red bell pepper, chopped
1 ripe avocado, chopped
2 Persian cucumbers, chopped
1 cup carrots, chopped or grated
1 cup basil leaves, torn
½ cup mint leaves, torn
¼ cup cilantro, torn
½ cup salted peanuts, crushed

Dressing

¼ cup creamy peanut butter
1 tablespoon plus 1 teaspoon tamari or soy
    sauce
1 tablespoon lime juice
2 teaspoons honey
1 teaspoon grated ginger
1 teaspoon red pepper flakes
Dash of rice vinegar
Sea salt and black pepper

I came up with this recipe when trying to make spring rolls for the first time (YouTube made it look so easy!) and failed miserably. But I had all the veggies chopped and ready, so I pivoted and made it into a salad that was actually kind of incredible.

1. Combine the cabbage, bell pepper, avocado, cucumbers, carrots, basil, mint, and cilantro in a large serving bowl.

2. Make the sauce: Mix the peanut butter, tamari, lime juice, honey, ginger, red pepper flakes, vinegar, salt, and pepper in a small bowl with a whisk or in a blender. Add water, 1 teaspoon at a time, until it reaches your desired consistency. (I prefer it to pour easily out of the blender, which usually takes about 3 teaspoons of water.)

3. Pour dressing over the salad and mix it up. Top with crushed peanuts.

Savory Crispy Carrot Fries

Cross-Pollination

4 large carrots, peeled and cut
    into 4 x ½-inch strips
1 teaspoon garlic powder
1 teaspoon onion powder
1 teaspoon paprika
1 teaspoon sea salt
½ teaspoon black pepper
2 tablespoons olive oil
2 tablespoons chopped parsley

Dipping Sauce

½ cup sour cream
½ cup plain Greek yogurt
1 tablespoon lemon juice
3 tablespoons chopped chives, plus more
    for serving
¼ teaspoon sea salt
¼ teaspoon black pepper

A healthier, mouthwatering, beta-carotene-packed alternative to satisfy your French fry craving, these carrot fries are crispy, salty, and especially satisfying when served with the creamy chive dip. Skip the deep fryer and bake them in the oven.

1. Preheat the oven to 425°F. Line a baking sheet with parchment paper.

2. Place the carrots, garlic powder, onion powder, paprika, salt, and pepper in a large bowl and toss with tongs until the carrots are well coated.

3. Place the carrots on the baking sheet in one layer, making sure they don't touch each other. Drizzle the olive oil over the carrots.

4. Bake for 25 to 30 minutes, flipping halfway, until the carrot fries are crispy and browned.

5. While the carrots are cooking, make the dipping sauce. Mix the sour cream, yogurt, lemon juice, chives, salt, and pepper together in a medium bowl. Top with more chopped chives. Set aside until you're ready to serve.

6. Place the carrot fries on a platter. Top with parsley and serve immediately with dipping sauce.

Slow Cooker Chicken

with Honeyed Carrots & Potatoes

Cross-Pollination

2 tablespoons olive oil

4 medium bone-in, skin-on chicken breasts
or thighs

5 to 6 large carrots, peeled and cut into
½-inch rounds

1 large yellow onion, roughly chopped

1 pound baby potatoes, quartered

½ cup salted butter, melted

⅓ cup honey

6 garlic cloves, minced or pressed

1 teaspoon dried parsley

1 teaspoon sea salt

¼ teaspoon black pepper

¼ teaspoon red pepper flakes

4 to 5 rosemary sprigs

1 cup chicken broth or water

A weeknight dinner that you can throw in the slow cooker in the morning and not think about for the rest of the day is my kind of jam. A hint of sweetness pairs with savory flavors to create a dish you'll add to your list of regulars. If your slow cooker has a sauté function, you can do this all in one pot.

1. Heat the olive oil in a large saucepan over medium heat. Sauté the chicken in the oil until lightly browned, about 3 minutes on each side.

2. Add the carrots, onion, and potatoes to the slow cooker. Place the chicken on top of the veggies.

3. In a small bowl, mix the butter, honey, garlic, parsley, salt, pepper, and red pepper flakes.

4. Pour the mixture over the chicken and veggies and mix to combine, then add the rosemary. Pour the broth over everything.

5. Cook on high for 4 to 6 hours, until the chicken is cooked through.

6. Remove the chicken breasts and shred with a fork. Remove the rosemary sprigs and serve the chicken, potatoes, and carrots hot, spooning extra sauce over the dish.

Carrot Slaw

Cross-Pollination

5 to 6 medium carrots, peeled
½ medium red cabbage
½ sweet red apple
3 scallions, thinly sliced
¼ cup finely chopped parsley

Dressing
¼ cup extra virgin olive oil
3 tablespoons apple cider vinegar
Juice of 1 lemon
2 tablespoons honey
2 teaspoons Dijon mustard
1 garlic clove, minced or pressed
1 teaspoon sea salt
½ teaspoon black pepper

When I was pregnant with my son, Luca, I couldn't get enough of this slaw. I would make it every other day and serve it on salads, over any protein, and eat it straight from the bowl as a snack. It's so simple but so insanely tasty.

1. Working in batches, place the carrots, cabbage, and apple in a food processor and chop in one-second intervals until the veggies are finely chopped but not mushy.

2. Make the dressing: Mix the olive oil, vinegar, lemon juice, honey, mustard, garlic, salt, and pepper together in a large bowl until well combined.

3. Transfer the carrots, cabbage, and apple mixture to the bowl along with the scallions and parsley and toss well to coat.

4. Taste and add salt or pepper as desired. Enjoy it cold.

PEPPERS

Anel's
Pepper Tips

Ideal planting time

Don't plant your peppers too early in the season; wait until the soil is 60°F or warmer. Bell peppers are very sensitive to cold temperatures and frost, so consider using row covers or cloths to protect the plants in late spring on colder days or if you're expecting a late frost.

When to harvest

Peppers can be harvested as soon as the plant is mature, and it's important to not let the fruit hang for too long. If that happens, the plant will stop producing fruit. Cut carefully with a knife or clippers rather than yanking the peppers off. Pepper plants aren't very sturdy, so you don't want to damage the stems. They will continuously produce fruit until it gets cold. So be sure to continue harvesting!

1. There are many varieties of peppers, and I encourage you to experiment with them! I always go with the classic bell peppers in every color, and each year I like to add some heat to the mix, with cayenne, habanero, serrano, and Thai chili peppers. Recently, shishito peppers have become one of my favorites, because they are super easy to grow and are delicious.

2. To prevent soil-borne disease, rotate your bell pepper crops to different areas of the garden each year. Be sure to keep them away from other nightshade-family plants, such as tomatoes, potatoes, and eggplant, to prevent the spread of disease and pests.

3. Pruning is very important for bell peppers. They often develop too many branches and flowers. Prune some of the small or lower-quality flowers and fruits in the beginning of the season so that the plant can develop a strong root system and have more energy to support heavier, bigger, and healthier peppers.

4. Two issues to look out for: If you notice that the flowers are drying up and falling off the plant, that's most likely due to extreme weather. They don't like the cold, but they also aren't fans of long periods of hot temperatures. You can provide temporary shade structures to protect them from intense heat and sunlight. You also might see that the leaf color is pale and growth is slow, which is usually a sign to feed the peppers with liquid fish or seaweed fertilizer.

5. Bell peppers thrive in warm soil conditions. Consider using a reflective mulcher, such as silver or white plastic, around the base of the plants. Reflective mulch can help with more light exposure to the lower leaves and soil, promoting better growth and earlier fruit development.

Offshoot
Oven-Roasted Red Peppers

If you think store-bought roasted red peppers are good, your mind will be blown when you make them at home. The flavor is rich and bitter and perfect.

4 medium-to-large red bell peppers, stemmed, seeded, and sliced into thick strips
1 teaspoon sea salt
¼ cup extra virgin olive oil

1. Preheat the oven to 450°F. Line a large baking sheet with parchment paper.

2. Place the pepper slices, skin side up, on the baking sheet.

3. Roast for 25 to 35 minutes, flipping halfway, until the peppers are soft and the skin begins to blister and turn black.

4. Transfer the roasted peppers to a large bowl and tightly cover. Let the peppers steam and cool to room temperature, 20 to 30 minutes.

5. Peel the skin off each pepper and discard.

6. Place the peppers in a jar with salt and olive oil and give them a good stir.

7. Refrigerate and enjoy for up to two weeks.

Shakshuka

Cross-Pollination

2 tablespoons olive oil

1 yellow onion, chopped

1 red, orange, or yellow bell pepper, chopped

3 garlic cloves, minced

One 28-ounce can diced tomatoes

1½ teaspoons ground cumin

1 teaspoon paprika

Sea salt and black pepper

6 ounces goat cheese or crumbled feta

6 large eggs

Chopped fresh herbs, like chives, dill, or parsley

Hot sauce, optional

The ultimate breakfast-for-dinner (or breakfast-for-breakfast) recipe incorporates lots of garden veggies in addition to peppers. It might look intimidating, but it's easier to make than you'd think and always impresses a crowd. I like to serve it with crusty buttered toast and a drizzle of hot sauce.

1. Preheat the oven to 375°F.

2. Heat the olive oil in a large cast-iron skillet over medium heat. Add the onion and bell pepper. Cook until soft, 10 to 15 minutes.

3. Add the garlic and cook until fragrant, stirring constantly, 1 minute.

4. Add the tomatoes and their juices, cumin, and paprika, and season lightly with salt and pepper. Simmer for about 10 minutes to thicken the tomatoes (don't skip this; it makes a difference).

5. Stir in the cheese. Crack the eggs over the mixture and season them with salt and pepper.

6. Transfer your skillet to the oven and bake for 8 to 10 minutes, until the eggs are set but still runny. Remove the skillet and sprinkle with fresh herbs. Top with hot sauce if desired.

Cowboy Caviar

Cross-Pollination

One 15-ounce can black beans, drained
    and rinsed

One 15-ounce can black-eyed peas,
    drained and rinsed

3 medium tomatoes or 20 baby tomatoes,
    diced

1 medium bell pepper, any color, seeded
    and diced

1 cup fresh corn kernels or frozen corn
    kernels, thawed and drained

½ medium red onion, finely diced

½ jalapeño, seeded and diced, optional

½ cup chopped cilantro leaves, plus more
    for serving

1 medium ripe avocado, pitted and diced

4 scallions, thinly sliced, greens only

Tortilla chips, for serving

Dressing

⅓ cup olive oil

¼ cup red wine vinegar

Juice of 1 lime

1 garlic clove, minced

1 teaspoon honey

1 teaspoon sea salt

½ teaspoon black pepper

Be warned: Once you start eating this dip, you won't be able to stop! My son treats it like a stew, eating it with a spoon straight from the bowl, but the rest of us enjoy this fresh and healthy dip with crunchy, salty tortilla chips. It comes together in 15 minutes and is a great way to use up a ton of produce.

1. In a large bowl, mix the beans, black-eyed peas, tomatoes, pepper, corn, onion, jalapeño, and cilantro. Set aside.

2. Make the dressing: Place the olive oil, vinegar, lime juice, garlic, honey, salt, and pepper in a mason jar and shake well to combine.

3. Pour the dressing over the veggie mixture and toss to combine. Cover the bowl and refrigerate for at least an hour before serving.

4. When you're ready to serve, add the avocado and toss to combine once more. Taste and add more salt and pepper as needed.

5. Garnish with cilantro leaves and scallion greens. Serve with tortilla chips.

Italian Stuffed Peppers

Cross-Pollination

4 large bell peppers, any color, stemmed, seeded, and halved vertically
2 teaspoons extra virgin olive oil
1 medium onion, diced
1 teaspoon sea salt, divided
3 garlic cloves, minced or pressed
1 pound ground turkey, beef, or chicken
½ teaspoon dried basil
½ teaspoon dried oregano
¼ teaspoon red pepper flakes
One 14-ounce can diced tomatoes
2 cups cooked quinoa
1 cup shredded mozzarella, divided
½ cup Parmesan
2 tablespoons chopped basil

A delectable, savory mix of ground meat, herbs, cheese, and quinoa are placed into sweet bell peppers for a cute and colorful meal with only 20 minutes of prep. Swap in Italian sausage (or chicken sausage) for a fun twist.

1. Preheat the oven to 375°F. Line a large baking sheet with parchment paper.

2. Arrange the pepper halves, cut sides up, on the baking sheet. Set aside.

3. Heat the olive oil in a large skillet over medium-high heat. Add the onions and ½ teaspoon of salt and cook until translucent, 5 to 7 minutes. Add the garlic and cook until fragrant, 1 more minute.

4. Add the meat, dried basil, dried oregano, remaining ½ teaspoon salt, and red pepper flakes. Cook, breaking apart the meat, until browned and cooked through, 5 to 7 minutes. Add the tomatoes and simmer for 1 more minute, stirring to combine.

5. Remove the pan from the heat and stir in the quinoa, ½ cup mozzarella, and the Parmesan.

6. Fill each pepper half with the meat mixture, then top with the remaining mozzarella.

7. Bake for 30 to 35 minutes, until the peppers are tender and the cheese is melted.

8. Garnish with fresh basil. Serve hot.

Sausage & Pepper Sandwiches

Cross-Pollination

3 tablespoons extra virgin olive oil

6 sweet or hot Italian sausages, halved and
    sliced lengthwise

3 bell peppers, seeded and sliced

1 large yellow onion, sliced

Sea salt and black pepper

2 garlic cloves, minced or pressed

2 teaspoons dried oregano

1 teaspoon dried basil

1 tablespoon tomato paste

1 teaspoon red pepper flakes

4 to 6 Italian rolls, optional

When my Nana's kitchen smelled like sausage and peppers, you knew it was going to be a great meal. To me, this smells like home and childhood, and it brings back a flood of memories. Nana used to serve hers in a bowl, but I prefer this dish as a sandwich. Either way, you can't go wrong.

1. Heat the olive oil in a large skillet over medium heat. Add the sausage and cook until brown on both sides, 8 to 10 minutes. Remove the sausage from the pan with a slotted spoon and set aside on a paper towel-lined plate. Keep the oil in the pan.

2. Add the peppers, onions, salt, and pepper to the pan, and cook, stirring occasionally, until the peppers are soft and the onions are translucent, 5 to 7 minutes.

3. Add the garlic, oregano, and basil, and stir to combine. Add the tomato paste and red pepper flakes and stir with a wooden spoon, scraping up any browned bits on the bottom of the pan.

4. Stir in the sausage and cook everything together for 1 minute.

5. Using tongs, place the sausage, pepper, and onion mix into a roll, if desired.

Chicken Cacciatore

Cross-Pollination

6 boneless, skinless chicken thighs, patted dry
2½ teaspoons sea salt, divided
½ teaspoon black pepper
½ cup all-purpose flour
3 tablespoons extra virgin olive oil
1 medium yellow onion, chopped
2 bell peppers, chopped
1 cup sliced cremini mushrooms
3 to 5 garlic cloves, minced or pressed
¾ cup dry white wine
One 14-ounce can crushed tomatoes
¾ cup chicken broth
1 tablespoon tomato paste
1 teaspoon dried basil
1 teaspoon dried oregano
1 pound spaghetti or linguine, optional
Grated Parmesan, optional
¼ cup fresh basil, roughly chopped

Note

To make this in a slow cooker, complete steps 1 through 3, then transfer the chicken and all other ingredients except for the pasta, Parmesan, and fresh basil to a slow cooker and cook on high for 4 hours. Cook the pasta separately, then serve with Parmesan and basil.

A restaurant-quality Italian classic that is a breeze to make at home. It's great for family dinners, and you can easily make it in a larger batch for a dinner party. I serve this stewy, soupy chicken dish over pasta with a simple arugula salad.

1. Season both sides of the chicken with 1 teaspoon of salt and the black pepper.

2. Place the flour on a large plate and dredge the chicken pieces in the flour, coating all over.

3. Heat the olive oil in a large pot or Dutch oven over medium-high heat. Add the chicken in one layer (you may need to work in batches). Cook the chicken until browned on one side, 5 to 6 minutes. Flip and cook on the other side until lightly browned, 2 more minutes.

4. Transfer the chicken to a plate and set aside. Repeat with the remaining chicken if necessary. Cut the chicken into smaller pieces, if desired.

5. Reduce the heat to medium-low and add the onions to the pot. Stir occasionally, until soft and translucent, 5 to 7 minutes.

6. Add the peppers and mushrooms and cook, stirring occasionally until they begin to soften, 5 to 7 minutes. Add the garlic and cook until fragrant, 1 more minute, stirring constantly.

7. Turn the heat to high and add the wine. Bring to a boil, stirring to scrape up the brown bits from the pan. Cook until the wine has mostly evaporated, about 5 minutes.

8. Add the crushed tomatoes, chicken broth, tomato paste, basil, oregano, and the remaining salt. Bring to a boil again, then reduce the heat to low and gently simmer until the sauce begins to reduce, 10 minutes.

9. Add the chicken back to the pot and spoon some of the sauce over it. Simmer on low heat until the chicken cooks through, at least 30 minutes but up to 60 minutes, depending on how much time you have. The longer you cook it, the deeper the flavors will become.

10. Serve in a large bowl over pasta, if desired. Top with Parmesan if desired, and garnish with chopped fresh basil.

Vegetarian Chili

Cross-Pollination

1 tablespoon extra virgin olive oil
1 yellow onion, chopped
2 bell peppers, seeded and finely chopped
Two 15-ounce cans black beans, rinsed
    and drained, divided
One 4-ounce can mild green chiles
4 garlic cloves, minced or pressed
2 tablespoons chili powder
1 tablespoon ground cumin
½ teaspoon dried oregano
½ teaspoon paprika
½ teaspoon sea salt, plus more to taste
½ teaspoon black pepper, plus more
    to taste
One 28-ounce can diced tomatoes
1 cup vegetable broth or water
One 15-ounce can kidney beans, rinsed
    and drained
1 cup frozen corn
¼ cup cilantro, roughly chopped
Juice of 1 lime

For Serving
Tortilla chips
Shredded cheddar
Avocado slices
Lime wedges
Chopped chives or scallions
Chopped cilantro
Sour cream
Corn bread

Chili is a comfort food in my home, but you don't need meat to make it fantastic. This smoky, flavorful vegetarian chili hits the spot on a rainy day and gets even better as leftovers.

1. In a large Dutch oven or pot, heat the olive oil over medium heat. Add the onion and bell peppers. Cook, stirring occasionally, until the peppers are soft and the onion is translucent, 7 to 10 minutes.

2. While the veggies are cooking, transfer one can of black beans to a blender and blend until smooth.

3. Add the chiles, garlic, chili powder, cumin, oregano, paprika, salt, and black pepper to the pot and cook, stirring constantly for 1 more minute.

4. Add the diced tomatoes, vegetable broth, black beans (blended and whole) and kidney beans and stir gently to combine. Partially cover, then simmer for 30 to 35 minutes, stirring occasionally.

5. Gently stir in the corn and cook until heated through, another 5 to 10 minutes.

6. Turn off the heat, then add the cilantro and lime juice. Stir and let sit for a few minutes before serving. Taste and add salt and black pepper as needed.

7. Serve in bowls with toppings or accompaniments of your choice.

Ajvar

Bosnian Roasted Pepper & Eggplant Spread

Cross-Pollination

4 medium red bell peppers, seeded and halved
1 medium eggplant, cut into 2-inch rounds
⅓ cup olive oil
4 garlic cloves, minced or pressed
2 teaspoons white wine vinegar
1 teaspoon sea salt, plus more to taste
½ teaspoon black pepper, plus more to taste

Bosnians love their ajvar. When I met Anel's family, I quickly learned that this smoky, tangy pepper and eggplant dip would be set on the table with every meal. They eat it with meat, bread, eggs, and pretty much anything else you could think of. The store-bought versions are pretty good, but homemade ajvar is magic.

1. Preheat the oven to 450°F. Line a large baking sheet with parchment paper.

2. Place the bell peppers and eggplant on the baking sheet in a single layer.

3. Bake for 50 to 60 minutes, turning halfway through, until the eggplant and peppers look almost black.

4. Remove the peppers and eggplant from the oven and set aside, covered, for 20 minutes to cool and steam slightly. Once they've cooled enough to touch, remove the skins from the eggplant and discard.

5. Add the peppers, eggplant, olive oil, garlic, vinegar, salt, and black pepper to a food processor. Pulse until the consistency is mostly smooth with some chunks.

6. Transfer the mixture to a medium saucepan and place over low heat.

7. Simmer for an hour, stirring every 15 minutes or so, until the sauce begins to thicken.

8. Taste and add more salt and/or black pepper as needed.

Note

You can also use the grill to achieve a smokier flavor. To do this, preheat the grill to 450°F and grill the peppers and eggplant until charred, 30 minutes, flipping halfway through. The char from the grill adds a great element of flavor. Then start with step 4.

Sheet Pan Chicken Fajita Bowls

Cross-Pollination

1 pound chicken breast, cut into
    thin strips
2 medium bell peppers, cut into
    thin strips
1 medium yellow onion, sliced
1 medium red onion, sliced
¼ cup olive oil
1 teaspoon chili powder
1 teaspoon ground cumin
1 teaspoon garlic powder
½ teaspoon paprika
½ teaspoon sea salt
¼ teaspoon black pepper
¼ cup chopped fresh cilantro leaves
2 limes
4 cups cooked brown or white rice

Toppings
Sliced avocado
Pico de gallo
Sour cream
Shredded cheddar
Cilantro leaves

This hearty and quick weeknight dinner is packed with the flavors of Mexican spices, sweet peppers and onions, bright lime, and fresh cilantro. You can serve it over rice, with tortillas, or on its own.

1. Preheat the oven to 425°F. Line a baking sheet with parchment paper.

2. Place the chicken strips, bell peppers, and onions in a single layer on the baking sheet.

3. In a small bowl, combine the olive oil, chili powder, cumin, garlic powder, paprika, salt, and black pepper. Drizzle the oil mixture over the chicken and veggies.

4. Bake for 20 to 25 minutes, until the chicken is completely cooked through and the veggies are slightly tender.

5. Add the cilantro and juice of one lime to the sheet pan and toss to combine. Taste and add more salt as needed.

6. Cut the other lime into wedges.

7. Serve the fajitas over rice and top with your choice of toppings and a lime wedge on the side.

Stuffed Pepper Casserole

Cross-Pollination

Cooking spray
1 pound lean ground beef or
    ground turkey
2 tablespoons extra virgin olive oil
2 medium bell peppers, seeded and
    chopped
1 medium yellow onion, chopped
3 garlic cloves, minced or pressed
1 jalapeño, seeded and chopped, optional
1 tablespoon tomato paste
1 teaspoon ground cumin
1 teaspoon chili powder
1 teaspoon sea salt
½ teaspoon dried oregano
¼ teaspoon black pepper
One 14-ounce can diced tomatoes
2 cups beef broth or water
1 tablespoon fresh lime juice
1 cup white rice
2 cups shredded cheddar, divided
2 tablespoons chopped cilantro

Get that delicious stuffed pepper flavor without stuffing a single pepper. This dish is a great family-friendly meal that comes together without a lot of effort.

1. Preheat the oven to 375° F. Spray a 9 x 13-inch casserole dish with cooking spray.

2. Place the beef in a medium pan over medium-high heat and cook, stirring and breaking up the meat, until mostly brown, 3 to 5 minutes. Remove from the pan and set aside.

3. Heat the oil in the same pan over medium heat and add the bell peppers and onion. Cook until the onion is translucent, 5 to 7 minutes.

4. Add the garlic, jalapeño (if using), and tomato paste, and cook until fragrant, 1 more minute. Add the cumin, chili powder, salt, oregano, and black pepper and give it a good stir.

5. Add the diced tomatoes, broth, lime juice, rice, and 1 cup of cheese, stir to combine, and transfer the mixture to the casserole dish.

6. Cover with foil and bake for 30 minutes.

7. Top with the remaining 1 cup of cheese and bake, uncovered, for 10 to 15 more minutes, until the cheese is melted and bubbling.

8. Remove from the oven and let cool for about 10 minutes before serving. Top with fresh cilantro.

Grilled Veggie Skewers

Cross-Pollination

4 to 6 baby red potatoes, quartered
1 red bell pepper, seeded and cut into
    1-inch pieces
1 yellow bell pepper, cut into 1-inch pieces
1 medium red onion, cut into 1-inch pieces
1 medium yellow onion, cut into
    1-inch pieces
1 medium zucchini, cut into rounds
1 to 2 tablespoons olive oil
Sea salt and black pepper

This recipe can be made a million different ways. I love grilled onions, so I always include two types. I'm not a fan of grilled green bell peppers, so I stick with red and yellow, but you can switch it up with any of your favorite veggies. We throw some version of these skewers on the grill a few times per week during grilling months.

1. If you're using wooden skewers, soak them in a large bowl of water while prepping your vegetables. This will prevent them from burning on the grill.

2. Preheat the grill to medium-high heat.

3. Skewer the vegetables in layers, making sure to leave room on each end for flipping.

4. Lay the skewers on a baking sheet and drizzle with olive oil to lightly coat. Sprinkle salt and pepper on each side.

5. Grill for 10 to 15 minutes, flipping halfway, until the vegetables are soft and you can see grill marks.

Note

These grilled veggies pair perfectly with Herby Chimichurri (page 139). If you don't own a grill or prefer to cook indoors, bake the skewers in the oven at 400°F for 15 to 20 minutes, turning halfway.

Pepper "Nachos"

Cross-Pollination

10 mini bell peppers, stemmed, halved, and seeded
1 tablespoon olive oil
1 pound ground beef, turkey, or meat alternative
1 tablespoon chili powder
½ teaspoon ground cumin
½ teaspoon garlic powder
½ teaspoon onion powder
¼ teaspoon sea salt
½ cup black beans, rinsed and drained
½ cup frozen corn
1 cup shredded cheddar
1 jalapeño, sliced, optional
Cilantro leaves

Swapping out tortilla chips for peppers will satisfy your nacho cravings with a healthier option bursting with color and flavor. These pepper nachos are a great way to get kids to eat more veggies and are fun to serve as an appetizer with friends.

1. Preheat the oven to 350°F. Line a baking sheet with parchment paper.

2. Add the pepper halves ("chips") to the baking sheet in one layer and set aside.

3. Heat the oil in a large skillet over medium-high heat. Add the meat and cook, stirring and breaking it up with a wooden spoon until it's fully cooked with no pink remaining, 7 to 10 minutes.

4. Add the chili powder, cumin, garlic powder, onion powder, and salt, and give it a good stir. Add the beans and cook for 2 more minutes, stirring occasionally. Add the corn and cook for another minute.

5. Spoon the meat mixture carefully over each pepper chip. Sprinkle each chip with cheese and top with a jalapeño slice, if desired.

6. Bake for 12 to 15 minutes, until the cheese is melted and the peppers are soft.

7. Top each pepper chip with a cilantro leaf and serve immediately.

Bosnian Sataraš

Cross-Pollination

3 tablespoons vegetable oil
3 bell peppers, any color, chopped
2 medium carrots, chopped
2 yellow onions, chopped
5 to 6 garlic cloves, chopped
¾ cup white rice, rinsed
2 teaspoons sea salt
1 teaspoon black pepper
1 teaspoon dried parsley
¼ cup chopped dill

My mother-in-law has been cooking this traditional Bosnian rice and vegetable dish since her mother taught her as a child. Living on a farm, they would use whatever vegetables they had on hand. She makes it for us every week, and it has become a comfort food for me over the last decade.

1. Heat the oil in a large pan over medium-high heat.
2. Add the peppers, carrots, and onions and cook, stirring occasionally, until the onions are translucent, 6 to 8 minutes.
3. Add the garlic and cook, stirring constantly until fragrant, for another minute.
4. Add 1 cup water and the rice and stir to combine.
5. Season with salt, pepper, and parsley and stir to combine once more.
6. Reduce the heat to low and simmer, covered, for 20 to 30 minutes, until the rice is fully cooked.
7. Add the dill, stir to combine, and serve hot.

BERRIES

Anel's

Berry Tips

Ideal planting time

Plant your berries in spring, after the last frost. Berries are perennials, meaning that they regrow every year with proper maintenance, so there's no need to replant them year after year. Birds will eat every last berry if you don't cover them with some kind of netting before they fully mature.

When to harvest

Pick your berries twice a week when they are ripe. Pick ripe raspberries and blackberries, cutting the shoot from the fruit after picking. Harvest blueberries by holding a container underneath and tickling/tapping the branch so they drop. Even if they are blue, that doesn't mean they're fully ripe.

1. Berries thrive in a lower pH (higher acidity) than vegetables, ideally between 3.5 and 5.5. Adding peat moss, rotted leaves, and composted pine bark to the soil around berry plants is the best way to add acidity to the soil. Avoid lime and wood ash, as they are alkaline and will increase the pH.

2. Plant berry plants 5 feet apart and about 4 inches deep. Use pine needles and bark as mulch. Rub off the flower buds to enable the plant to develop good roots.

3. The most important part of growing berries is keeping them pruned, but different types of berries have different pruning techniques and schedules. It's important to understand the pruning requirements of each berry plant you're growing. Regular and correct pruning can lead to a bigger harvest, larger fruit, and better flavor.

4. When growing blackberries, cut the plant to 3 feet tall mid-summer to encourage the growth of lateral branches, which bear more fruit. Then, in late winter/early spring, cut all of the lateral branches to about half their length.

5. Strawberries are an invasive plant. At the end of summer, they spread by throwing shoots out away from the plant to develop new ones. For the first two years, you want to prevent this by cutting off the shoots before they develop into new plants, so that they don't take nutrients from the original plant. After two years, allow the shoots to become new plants, cut them from the old plants, and remove the old plants from the garden.

 **Offshoot**
Berry Simple Syrup

Flavored simple syrups can be used for more than just cocktails. I use them for fancy mocktails or even just a splash in some seltzer with lunch. They can be drizzled over ice cream or pancakes and waffles for a little bit of added excitement.

2 cups fresh or frozen berries
1 cup sugar
1 teaspoon lemon juice

1. Place the berries, sugar, lemon juice, and 1 cup water in a medium saucepan over medium heat. Simmer, stirring occasionally, until the sugar has completely dissolved, about 2 minutes.

2. With a wooden spoon, mash up the berries and let the mixture simmer, stirring occasionally until the berries have broken down and the sauce begins to thicken, 15 to 20 minutes.

3. Remove the saucepan from the heat and let cool for 15 to 20 minutes.

4. Strain the syrup into an airtight bottle or container and refrigerate for up to 2 weeks.

Easy Berry Pie

1 frozen pie crust
2 tablespoons strawberry jam
2 tablespoons lemon juice
3 cups strawberries, chopped
1½ cups blueberries
1 package cream cheese, room
    temperature
¼ cup confectioners' sugar
2 cups sweetened whipped cream

This tasty pie, which takes only 10 minutes to assemble, will become an instant hit in your house this summer. It is the ultimate summer-holiday dessert: bright, colorful, sweet, and a hit with every age.

1. Bake the pie crust according to package directions.

2. While the crust is baking, whisk the jam and lemon juice together in a large bowl. Add the berries and toss to coat.

3. With an electric mixer or stand mixer, beat the cream cheese and sugar until smooth in a medium bowl. Add the whipped cream and beat to combine.

4. Spread the cream cheese mixture onto the cooled pie crust and top with the berries. Lightly stir the cream cheese with the berry mixture to combine.

5. Transfer to the refrigerator for at least 20 minutes and serve cold.

Any-Berry Jam

1 pound fresh berries (see Note 1), sliced
1½ cups sugar
½ teaspoon lemon zest
1 tablespoon lemon juice

During the height of the pandemic, we went strawberry picking as a family. We were antsy to get out of the house, and strawberry picking was outside, where we could socially distance. Four pounds of strawberries ended up in our kitchen and after giving away a bunch of them, I decided to try making jam for the first time. It's now one of my favorite treats to make and gift to friends and family. It's a lot easier than you would think, and it tastes so much better when it's homemade.

1. Add berries and sugar to a large pan over medium heat. Bring to a boil, stirring constantly and mashing down the berries so that they fully break down.

2. Add the lemon zest and juice and simmer on medium heat until the jam thickens, 20 to 25 minutes, stirring often to ensure that the jam doesn't burn.

3. If it foams, scoop the foam off the top and discard.

4. Pour into a glass jar and let cool at room temperature.

5. Cover and refrigerate (see Note 2) or use as soon as it's cool.

Notes

1. One pound of fresh berries equals about 18 to 20 medium strawberries, 3 cups of blueberries, 4 cups of raspberries, or 3 cups of blackberries.
2. This jam can be stored in the refrigerator in an airtight container for up to 3 weeks...if it lasts that long!

All-the-Berry Crumble

Cross-Pollination

Crumble

8 tablespoons unsalted butter, room
    temperature, cubed, plus more for
    greasing
1 cup rolled oats
½ cup brown sugar
¼ cup granulated sugar
¼ cup all-purpose flour
½ teaspoon ground cinnamon
½ teaspoon sea salt

Berry Filling

2 cups blueberries
1 cup blackberries
1 cup strawberries
1 cup raspberries
1 tablespoon cornstarch
⅓ cup sugar
Zest from 1 lemon
1 tablespoon lemon juice
¼ teaspoon sea salt

For Serving

Mint leaves
Vanilla ice cream, optional

This berry crumble, made with whatever berries you have in the garden or fridge, is a mix of sweet and tart, buttery and juicy, and crunchy and tender. Even the most amateur bakers can swing this one! I highly recommend serving it with a scoop of vanilla ice cream.

1. Preheat the oven to 375°F and grease a 9-inch square baking dish with butter.

2. Make the crumble: In a large bowl, mix the oats, brown sugar, granulated sugar, flour, cinnamon, and salt.

3. Add the cubed butter and mix in, breaking it up with a fork (or your fingers) until the mixture becomes coarse crumbs. Set aside.

4. Make the filling: Place the berries in the baking dish.

5. In a small bowl, mix the cornstarch, sugar, lemon zest, lemon juice, and salt.

6. Pour the sugar mixture over the berries and gently toss to coat. Sprinkle the crumble evenly over the berries.

7. Bake for 30 to 35 minutes, until the berries are bubbling and the crumble is golden brown.

8. Serve with a mint leaf on each serving and a scoop of ice cream, if desired.

Note

Use any mixture of berries, as long as it adds up to 5 cups. If you're only yielding one type in your garden, sub in frozen or store-bought berries to supplement.

Strawberry & Corn Salsa

Cross-Pollination

Zest and juice of 1 lime
1 teaspoon sea salt
½ teaspoon black pepper
1½ cups finely chopped strawberries
　(about 15 medium)
1 cup finely chopped tomatoes (10 to 15
　baby tomatoes or 3 to 4 medium
　tomatoes)
1 cup corn kernels (from 2 ears of corn;
　see Tip)
½ medium red onion, finely diced
¼ cup minced cilantro
1 jalapeño, seeded and minced
Tortilla chips, for serving

Light, fresh, sweet, savory, and a little spicy, this salsa works for both chip-dipping and taco-topping. If you can't handle the heat, skip the jalapeño.

1. In a large bowl, mix the lime zest, lime juice, salt, and pepper.
2. Add the strawberries, tomatoes, corn, onion, cilantro, and jalapeño, and stir to combine.
3. Taste and add more honey for sweetness, lime juice for tanginess, or salt for flavor.
4. Let the salsa sit for at least 20 minutes to marinate before serving with tortilla chips.

Tip

I use frozen corn here in a pinch.

My Kids' Favorite Smoothie Bowl

1 cup plain unsweetened Greek yogurt
1 tablespoon almond butter
1 frozen banana, peeled
1 cup berries of your choice
½ cup milk of your choice

Toppings

Mixed berries
Granola
Pomegranate seeds
Chopped or slivered almonds
Drizzle of almond or peanut butter
Banana slices
Chia seeds

There are a million ways you can make this smoothie bowl, and my kids go bananas for it (pun intended). They think it's ice cream, and I know it's not. Blend in a small handful of frozen spinach for some hidden nutrients, *wink wink*.

1. Add the yogurt, almond butter, banana, berries, and milk to a blender and blend until smooth but thicker than a smoothie.

2. Pour into bowls and top with your favorite toppings!

Berry Goat Cheese Spread

Cross-Pollination

1 cup berries of your choice, rinsed
    and drained
1 tablespoon lemon juice
Pinch of salt
2 tablespoons sugar
1 teaspoon fresh thyme leaves, plus more
    for serving
One 8-ounce goat cheese log, sliced into
    ½-inch rounds
Honey
Bread, crackers, or crostini, for serving

If you've made it this far, you know I love a good dip. This spread can be used on sandwiches, toasts, or put out in a bowl for a dipping appetizer. The color is stunning and will wow any crowd.

1. Add the berries, lemon juice, salt, and sugar to a medium saucepan over medium heat and cook until thickened, 5 to 7 minutes, stirring often.

2. Remove the berry mixture from the heat, pour into a medium bowl, and mash or stir until smooth. Mix in the thyme, then let the mixture cool at room temperature for 10 minutes.

3. Remove 2 tablespoons of the mixture for serving and store in a container in the refrigerator.

4. Add the goat cheese rounds to the bowl with the berry mixture and mix until just combined. It should be a little lumpy.

5. Place a 12-inch-wide piece of plastic wrap on your counter or work surface and pour the goat cheese mixture into the middle. Wrap the plastic wrap around the cheese to form a log and secure the ends. You may need a second piece of plastic wrap.

6. Place in the refrigerator for at least 1 hour until the cheese is firm and holds its shape.

7. Remove from the refrigerator 20 minutes before you're ready to serve. Top with the extra berry mixture, a drizzle of honey, and some fresh thyme leaves. Serve with bread, crackers, or crostini.

Blueberry Mint Cobbler

Cross-Pollination

6 tablespoons cold unsalted butter, thinly
    sliced, plus more for greasing
1 cup all-purpose flour, leveled
2 tablespoons cane sugar, plus more
    for sprinkling
2 teaspoons baking powder
Zest from ½ lemon
½ teaspoon sea salt
½ cup whole milk
1 tablespoon salted butter, melted
Vanilla ice cream

Berry Filling
4 cups fresh blueberries
¼ cup finely sliced mint leaves
¼ cup cane sugar
1 tablespoon all-purpose flour
1 tablespoon fresh lemon juice

This homemade dessert will have you coming back for seconds...and maybe thirds. It's rustic and simple to make, but I would buy it at any restaurant. The punch of mint adds an herbaceous note to this classic dessert and uses up what's bound to be your fastest growing herb in the garden.

1. Preheat the oven to 400°F. Grease a small baking dish with unsalted butter.

2. Make the filling: Place the blueberries, mint, sugar, and flour in a large bowl and toss to coat. Add the lemon juice and toss once more. Transfer the mixture to the baking dish and set aside.

3. Make the dough: In a large bowl, mix the flour, sugar, baking powder, lemon zest, and salt.

4. Add the unsalted butter and mix with your hands until well combined. Add the milk and continue mixing until it forms a thick dough.

5. Use an ice cream scoop to scoop the dough and form 2-inch rounds. Place the dough rounds on top of the blueberries, spacing them as evenly as possible.

6. Brush the melted butter over the dough rounds and sprinkle with sugar.

7. Bake for 30 to 35 minutes, until the biscuits are golden brown and the fruit is bubbling.

8. Cool for 10 to 15 minutes before serving. Serve warm, with a scoop of ice cream.

Blueberry Braised Brisket

Serves 4

Cross-Pollination

3 to 4 pounds beef brisket, trimmed
1 teaspoon sea salt
1 teaspoon black pepper
1 teaspoon dried parsley
2 tablespoons olive oil
2 medium yellow onions, roughly chopped
6 garlic cloves, minced or pressed
1 cup dry red wine
1 cup beef broth
2 cups fresh or frozen blueberries, divided
3 thyme sprigs, plus more for serving
⅓ cup balsamic vinegar
¼ cup brown sugar

A fun and unique twist on a classic slow-roasted brisket. It's smoky, sweet, rich, and comforting in the way that only briskets can be.

1. Preheat the oven to 325°F.

2. Sprinkle salt, pepper, and parsley on both sides of the brisket.

3. In a large oven-safe pot or Dutch oven, heat the olive oil over medium-high heat. Add the brisket and cook until lightly browned, 3 to 5 minutes per side. Transfer the brisket to a large plate.

4. In the same pot over medium-high heat, cook the onions until they are translucent, about 5 minutes, stirring occasionally. Add the garlic and cook until fragrant, about 1 more minute. Add the wine, broth, and 1 cup of blueberries and bring to a simmer, scraping down the sides and bottom of the pot.

5. Add the brisket back to the pot and bring the mixture to a boil. Place the thyme sprigs around the meat. Cover the pot and place it in the oven for 2 hours.

6. Remove the pot from the oven, add the vinegar, and gently stir to combine. Return the pot to the oven for 50 minutes to 1 hour, until the meat is very tender.

7. Remove the brisket from the pot and place it on a large cutting board, covered with foil, to cool for at least 10 minutes. Discard the thyme. When the brisket is cool enough to handle, cut it against the grain into thin slices, about ¼-inch thick.

8. Place the pot on the stove over low heat and simmer the sauce and onions until the sauce has reduced by half and begins to thicken, about 20 minutes.

9. Add the brown sugar and stir to combine. Add more salt and pepper to taste. Add the remaining blueberries and gently stir to combine.

10. Arrange the brisket slices on a large platter and drizzle the sauce and onions over them. Garnish with fresh thyme leaves.

Blueberry, Basil & Goat Cheese Salad

Cross-Pollination

1 cup arugula, roughly chopped
1 cup spinach, roughly chopped
½ cup basil, roughly chopped
3 scallions, greens only, chopped
1 cup blueberries
½ cup slivered almonds or whole almonds,
　　roughly chopped
4 ounces goat cheese, crumbled

Dressing
¾ cup extra virgin olive oil
¼ cup blueberries
2 tablespoons balsamic vinegar
1 teaspoon honey or maple syrup
Sea salt and black pepper

This fresh and healthy salad makes a great side dish out of seven simple ingredients. The blueberry and basil flavors stand out and pair perfectly with tangy goat cheese and lots of leafy greens. The simple blueberry dressing is lightly sweet and tart; use it on any of your favorite salads.

1. Make the dressing: Place the olive oil, blueberries, vinegar, honey, salt, and pepper in a blender or food processor and blend until smooth. Transfer to an airtight container and set aside.

2. Make the salad: Place the arugula, spinach, basil, and scallions in a large bowl.

3. Pour as much of the dressing as you like over the salad and mix well with tongs.

4. Add the blueberries, almonds, and goat cheese and gently mix once more. Serve immediately.

Note

If you have an abundance of strawberries or blackberries, substitute those in for the blueberries. You can make the dressing up to two days in advance and store in an airtight container in the fridge.

Blackberry Old-Fashioned

Cocktail + Mocktail

Serves 1

Cocktail

4 ounces bourbon or rye whiskey
½ cup blackberries, plus more for serving
½ teaspoon fresh squeezed lemon juice
3 teaspoons simple syrup
2 dashes Angostura bitters
Ice cubes
2 blackberries

Mocktail

1 black tea bag
½ cup blackberries, plus more for serving
½ teaspoon fresh squeezed lemon juice
2 teaspoons simple syrup
4 dashes Angostura bitters
Ice cubes
2 blackberries

Old-fashioneds are my husband's go-to drink order, and this blackberry version is his new favorite! I prefer the mocktail myself, but you can't go wrong either way. It's a great warm-weather whiskey cocktail with the ideal amount of light sweetness.

1. To make the mocktail only: Boil 2 cups of water and steep the tea bag for 3 to 5 minutes. Remove the tea bag and let the tea cool in the fridge until it's cold. This can be done ahead of time.

2. Place the blackberries, lemon juice, and simple syrup in a cocktail shaker and muddle until well mixed.

3. Add bourbon (cocktail) or tea (mocktail), bitters, and a handful of ice to the shaker. Shake until ice cold.

4. Place a large ice cube or a handful of ice into two glasses. Use a strainer to pour the cocktail over the ice. Garnish each drink with a blackberry.

Berry Avocado Smoothie

1 cup milk of your choice, plus more as
    needed
½ ripe avocado, peeled and pitted
½ banana, peeled
½ cup frozen mixed berries
1 tablespoon chia seeds, optional
1 teaspoon coconut oil, optional

I love using avocado to hide extra healthy fat in smoothies for the whole family. This Millennial-favorite fruit adds a yummy layer of creaminess and extra health benefits without much flavor so the berries and banana can shine.

1. Place the milk, avocado, banana, berries, chia seeds (if using), and coconut oil (if using) in a blender and blend until very smooth, about 1 minute.

2. Add more milk depending on your preferred thickness.

3. Serve immediately.

Berry Shrub

2 cups berries of your choice
2 cups sugar
1½ cups vinegar of your choice (I like apple cider or red wine)

First thing's first: We're talking about drinking vinegar here, not a bush on your lawn. The best part about making shrubs is that you can make them in any season, using virtually any berry, fruit, or herb and any type of vinegar that you have lying around. Add some to club soda for a refreshing mocktail and a pour of your go-to liquor for an adult beverage.

1. Place the berries in a large bowl and lightly mash with a fork. Pour the sugar over the berries and stir well to combine.

2. Tightly cover the bowl and let it sit at room temperature until the mixture looks juicy, 1 to 2 days, stirring once or twice.

3. Strain the fruit through a fine-mesh sieve over a medium bowl. Compost the fruit.

4. Add the vinegar to the syrup and stir to combine. Taste and add more vinegar or sugar to your preference.

5. Pour the shrub into a clean jar and cover. Let sit in the refrigerator for at least 3 days until the vinegar flavor mellows out.

Note

For a mocktail, pour 2 tablespoons of the shrub into a glass of ice and fill the rest with soda water. For a cocktail, add 1 ounce of tequila, vodka, or gin. Garnish with berries if desired.

Mixed Berry Muffins

with Honey Butter

Cooking spray, optional
2 cups all-purpose flour
¾ cup sugar
2 teaspoons baking powder
½ teaspoon sea salt
2 eggs
8 tablespoons unsalted butter, melted
½ cup milk of your choice
1 teaspoon vanilla extract
1 cup berries of your choice, rinsed
    and chopped

Honey Butter

8 tablespoons softened unsalted butter
3 tablespoons honey
¼ teaspoon sea salt

Everyone in the family will eat these muffins like it's their job. They are moist and sweet and bursting with flavor, and the honey butter takes them up a notch to make them perfect for a grab-and-go breakfast or after-school snack.

1. Preheat the oven to 400°F. Line a muffin pan with cupcake liners or spray with cooking spray.

2. Mix the flour, sugar, baking powder, and salt in a large bowl. Set aside.

3. Whisk the eggs, butter, milk, and vanilla in a medium bowl.

4. Add the egg mixture to the flour mixture and stir to combine. It might be a little lumpy—that's okay. Gently fold in the berries.

5. Spoon the batter into the muffin cups, about three-fourths of the way up.

6. Bake for 18 to 22 minutes or until lightly golden on top. Cool for a few minutes before serving.

7. Make the honey butter: Mix the butter, honey, and salt in a large bowl with a hand mixer until light and fluffy.

8. Transfer to a small bowl. Once the muffins have cooled, spread the honey butter on top to enjoy.

Index

Acknowledgments

So many people made this book, my dream project, a possibility:

To **Olivia Peluso**, the world's best editor. There are no words to express how grateful I am to have you in my life. You have become more than just an editor; you're a friend. From literal life-or-death experiences to many laughs on set, your positive attitude, dry, witty humor, and irreverent fashion choices make everything and every day working together more fun. I'm forever impressed by and grateful for your editing skills and will never forget how you were immediately drawn to **Garden Grown**, exactly as it is—embracing the book, my family, and the recipes from day one.

To everyone at DK who worked so hard to make it a reality. Especially **Bill Thomas** and the design team for your thoughtful designs and patience with my weirdly specific feedback. You took what was in my head and made it even more beautiful on paper.

To my literary agent, **Sally Ekus**, for believing in this book before anyone, and for taking a chance on me. You have taught me so much about the world of cookbooks and guided me in the right direction every step of the way. Knowing that you're on my team makes me feel safe and strong. Your fierce but gentle confidence, tenacity, and support will never be forgotten.

To **Kelly Matheis**, without whom I would never have finished this book. You keep me on track day by day, week by week, and make me belly laugh along the way. I am grateful for you, your insane organization skills, your daily humorous texts, and your friendship.

To **Julia Dags**, my partner in crime, surrogate little sister, and photographer extraordinaire. You have brought this book to life with your camera, talent, and passion for everything you put your hands on. You have an eye like no one else and should side hustle as a motivational speaker with all that positivity. I'm so lucky to call you a friend. JD²!

Nicolette Massaro, I don't know how you do it! You became a food stylist overnight, bringing out the beauty in every dish with your tiny tweezers, spray bottles, and magical vision. You make everything more fun.

To **Dana White**, for taking the time to thoroughly test these recipes and provide thoughtful and helpful feedback.

To **Kara Watson**, for being the very first person to help me see that this book was a possibility. You got the ball rolling, and

let's hope it never stops! Thank you for your friendship and guidance.

Jesse Straus, the fact that we're still friends after my endless design and art direction questions is a miracle. You're always there to lend a hand and do it with a smile on your face.

To the Lemon Stripes readers and followers, new and old, for sticking with me, embracing me and my family for who we are, and lifting me up throughout the years. Without you, this book wouldn't exist. I wish I could thank each and every one of you for your support and love across an internet that can sometimes be a very harsh place.

To my in-laws, **Isma** and **Ibro**, for being our village and helping with the kids, especially when I had to work on this book late at night or on the weekends, and for loving all of us unconditionally. Volim te puno.

Dad, thank you for teaching me to always follow my dreams, no matter how crazy they may seem. For encouraging me to be my best self and pushing me to do better. And for passing down your passion for and love of a well-cooked meal.

To my **mama**, who showed me what it meant to do it all. Your unwavering support of everything I've ever tried to do keeps me going. You taught me how to be a good mother while also having a life of my own, a lesson that I'm incredibly grateful for.

Lauren, life without you, sissy, wouldn't be life. Thank you for caring about every single meal I eat in a day, and for cheering me on with this book and everything I've ever done always and forever. And for making me feel like a 5-star chef whenever I cook you a meal.

To my babies, **Amalia** and **Luca**, for lighting up every day of my life. You inspire me to do better, to be better, and to do my part for your future. You'll never know, my loves, how much I love you.

And finally, the biggest thank you to my amazing husband, **Anel**. This book would not be possible without your incredible wealth of garden knowledge and your unyielding support. Thank you for testing all of my recipes and giving me your honest feedback...even when it felt a little too honest! You are the very best partner, cheerleader, supporter, and friend I could ever ask for. You are our number one dada, gardener, chicken daddy, and protector. Choosing you was the best choice I have ever made.

About the Author

Julia Dzafic is the founder and voice behind Lemon Stripes, a lifestyle blog with a focus on motherhood and healthy living. She lives in Westport, Connecticut, with her husband, Anel, their two children, Amalia and Luca, their pit mix, Boots, and a flock of chickens.

Visit her at lemonstripes.com.